SHATTERED
LOVE

SHATTERED LOVE

A MEMOIR

RICHARD CHAMBERLAIN

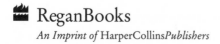 ReganBooks
An Imprint of HarperCollins*Publishers*

Grateful acknowledgment is made for permission to reprint the following copyrighted material:

Quote from *No Name on the Street* by James Baldwin, reprinted courtesy of the James Baldwin Estate.

Passage from *Light Upon Light: Inspiration from Rumi* by Andrew Harvey, published by North Atlantic Books. Copyright © 1996 by Andrew Harvey. Reprinted by permission of the publisher.

All photographs courtesy of Richard Chamberlain with the following exceptions, which are all used by permission: Insert page 6 (bottom) © Photofest; page 7 © 1969 Warner Bros.–Seven Arts, Inc., all rights reserved; page 9 (top left) © Photofest, (top right) © Metro Goldwyn Mayer Studios, (bottom) © Photofest; pages 10–11 courtesy of the Wolper Organization and Warner Bros.; page 12 (top) © Rosemont Productions, Ltd.; page 13 © Photofest; pages 14–15 (top) © 1985 Paramount Pictures, all rights reserved; page 16 courtesy of Jonas Morh/JME.

HarperCollins books may be purchased for educational, business, or sales promotional use. For information please write: Special Markets Department, HarperCollins Publishers Inc., 10 East 53rd Street, New York, NY 10022.

FIRST EDITION

Designed by Nancy Singer

Printed on acid-free paper

Library of Congress Cataloging-in-Publication Data has been applied for.

ISBN 0-06-008743-9

03 04 05 06 07 QN/QW 10 9 8 7 6 5 4 3

For Moani
with all my heart can give

THE WORLD OF ORIGIN

*Some people are glad when the rose breaks into blossom and fans
awake its secret splendor; some are glad when its petals fall
back and rejoin Origin.*

*Some people are happy when friendship, passion, belief, and
unbelief no longer exist, for then they can marry Origin and
live in its peace. Even the values we love and celebrate most
fervently can become walls between us and Him, darkened fountains
of narrowness, of duality.*

*The world of Origin is an always-flowing river of Breadth and Unity.
Long ago, tired of discriminations, I chose Unity as my
house and Breadth as the water of my ablutions.*

Long ago, exhausted by duality, I buried my head in the Sun.

*Long ago, worn to a husk by likes and dislikes, I died into the
Love that cannot die and that casts no shadow.*

> *Rumi*
> *(Translated by Andrew Harvey)*

PROLOGUE

I grew up in a single-story house, somewhat Mediterranean in style, fronted by a patio with high, thick walls. The outside wall met the house in an upward curve that formed a comfortable backrest for little kids like me who liked to sit on walls. Inside this corner an old ornamental walnut tree spread its branches over the terra-cotta tile roof, keeping the dining room cool.

As kids, we often climbed this nonproducing tree and charged around the patio walls and roof like demented monkeys, terrifying my mother, who would run out and urge us down to safer ground.

One hot afternoon, during summer vacation from grammar school, I wandered in the yard looking for something to do. None of my pals seemed to be around, and I was bored. For want of a better idea I climbed the walnut tree and sat on the wall, leaning back against the restful curve. A light summer breeze ruffled the leaves as I watched the occasional car or pedestrian pass on the street. I gazed up at the overhanging branches and hoped some of our local feathered friends—mockingbirds, blue jays, and doves—would come to visit me.

As I sat there motionless, something absolutely new happened to me. I was filled with total stillness. It was almost as if I wasn't even breathing, almost as if I'd become part of the wall, part of the tree. And in this stillness I was observing everything around me with complete neutrality, with no thought at all. There seemed to be observation, but no observer.

I don't know how long this lasted—probably not more than half an hour, possibly less. I did not know what was happening to me. I only know that my thinking went silent, and my sense of self disappeared. I experienced absolute simplicity and peace.

Of course I couldn't have described any of this at the time. At seven I had no context, no knowledge that would have allowed me to name and understand what was happening. I simply felt a vibrant, alert peace, and I loved the feeling.

I had no urge to talk about this experience with my parents or friends. But I did very much want it, whatever it was, to come back.

Several times after this magical day I climbed up and sat in the same place on the wall hoping to repeat the mysterious experience. It didn't come again. That is, it didn't come again in quite that way until a few days ago, over sixty years later.

THE CHAMBERLAIN
MAGIC SHOW

I was born in Los Angeles during the Great Depression and was quickly whisked off to Beverly Hills. Alas, it was to the normal, pre-90210 part of that glittering town, the "wrong" side of Wilshire Boulevard—and, even worse, the wrong side of Beverly Drive. In short, the wrong side of the now-vanished streetcar tracks.

My folks took out a thirty-five-year mortgage and bought a three-bedroom, one-and-a-quarter-bathroom house for a hefty seven thousand dollars. There were five of us: Chuck and Elsa, my father and mother; Bill, my brother; and soon Nonnie, my wonderful maternal grandmother.

There were no freeways, no tall buildings in L.A., no jet planes, no zip codes, no smog, no TV—and consequently no video games, no computers or cell phones, no drugs or guns at school. Some of our neighbors still had iceboxes instead of the newfangled fridges, so the ice truck trundled down our street every other day, delivering big blocks of ice. We kids used to clamor after the truck, begging for chunks to lick on hot summer days. The Good Humor man drove by too, ringing real bells. An ice cream bar cost five cents.

Who needed TV? We had the movies, at ten cents a double bill. And it was the golden age of radio—soap operas and music, dramas and news, on weekdays, and an extravaganza of comedy and variety shows on the weekends: Jack Benny, Bob Hope, Fred Allen, Red Skelton.

I loved listening to radio dramas and fairy tales and mysteries. Television scenes are limited by the varying skills of the actors, and especially by limited production budgets—you get only what the producers can afford. But my imagination had unlimited funds to spend on the images my radio evoked. And the picture tube in my head was widescreen, full color, and a hundred feet high.

There were vacant lots galore with tall grass to play in. We used to hide in the grass, pulling up clumps with dirt clods at the end and then lofting these missiles over where we thought our friends were hiding. When you got hit with one it didn't usually hurt that much. The neighborhood was full of kids, and even at preschool age we were free to roam and play and invent adventure. No kidnappers, no molesters, and no drug dealers—house and car doors left unlocked—we felt safe; we took safety for granted.

I was seven years old on that Day of Infamy when the Japanese bombed Pearl Harbor and savaged the U.S. Navy, awakening the Sleeping Giant and drawing us into mortal combat with the rampaging fascist forces of Germany, Japan, and Italy. Children pick up on just about everything, and my parents' initial shock at suddenly being at war scared my brother and me. Seeing this, they changed their tune and explained to us that the fighting was very, *very* far away, and that our brave and righteous military would keep us as safe and sound as we'd always been. Still believing that moms and dads speak only the truth, I bought this, and the war became in my juvenile imagination a distant high adventure, a rough-and-ready sporting event that we good guys were bound to win.

The war released a tremendous energy in the United States, which until then was still suffering the deprivations and gloom of the Depression. The accelerating war effort took on a youthful determination, a robust, vital innocence—we were so obviously the white-hatted heroes fighting valiantly against the black hats of darkness.

Even through our inevitable defeats and losses, Americans

remained feisty and optimistic. Our energetic optimism was apparent in our jive-filled, swinging music, and in our exuberant jitterbugging. Movies fortified our confidence in our superb fighting men and pumped up our loathing of the villainous Germans and Japanese (somehow the Italians never seemed that dangerous). If you have to march out and kill people, it's useful to hate them.

Our grammar school had paper drives and scrap metal drives. We kids would collect old newspapers all through our neighborhoods and pile the playground high with stacks of carefully tied bundles of the *Los Angeles Times* and huge piles of scrap. Once I took a fancy to a sort of Oscar-like shiny brass trophy on one of these piles, stole it, and took it home. When Dad saw it he asked where I'd gotten it. I lied, saying that I'd found it in the alley. He asked me to show him exactly where. I was mighty scared, but I took him out into the alley behind our house and pointed out with my shaking finger a particular trashcan. Dad, no fool drunk *or* sober, fixed me with a gaze of Olympian severity and asked again, "Where did you get it?" I admitted, stuttering, "The s-scrap pile." We returned home and I got spanked, more for lying than stealing.

Food was rationed with allotted food stamps. I remember that butter and sugar and meat and, worst of all, bubble gum were in particularly short supply. Margarine was easier to get, but the dairy companies got a law passed permitting the sale of only white margarine in large, unbutterlike chunks. To make this white stuff more appetizing, my grandmother would soften it in the oven and then mix in yellow coloring. The newly yellow margarine would be cooled in molds the shape of normal butter cubes. This was a tricky procedure because if the margarine actually melted it would separate and become an inedible mess.

Automakers were all making military vehicles—Jeeps and tanks and such—so new cars were just about impossible to find. By the end of the war my dad's old Ford had well over two hundred thousand miles on it. Car tires were difficult to replace (old ones were recycled), and gasoline was severely rationed. And yet the war remained "over there," and our lives went on pretty much as before.

For me the only really frightening aspects of the far-off fighting were the frequent air-raid warnings and nighttime blackouts. When the sirens sang, we had to turn out all our lights. Los Angeles became absolutely dark, invisible to enemy planes except for searchlights blazing into the sky, which might have given something away. My mother, block captain of our neighborhood militia, would go out and organize her bomb and fire squads. I remember one nighttime air-raid warning that seemed particularly real. I was in bed frightened to tears. Dad came in and told me our superfast P-38s were up in the sky and would surely shoot down enemy planes before they could even get close. It worked and I went to sleep. That's one of my rare good memories of Dad.

Another good memory was when Dad would drive me to Aunt Blanche's house somewhere in the downtown L.A. area. Normally, driving alone with Dad was extremely uncomfortable—I could never think of anything to say to this mythic, dark man, and I always felt silently disapproved of. But on the way to Aunt Blanche's there was a San Francisco–type steep hill with a special bump that, when traversed at high speed, would almost fling the old Ford airborne and make my stomach dance around weightlessly. Occasionally I could wheedle Dad into hitting the accelerator and giving me the thrill of being a part-time astronaut.

Beverly Vista, our local elementary school, was a five-minute walk from home. It was an excellent school, not yet strangled by bureaucracy. It had beautiful buildings, first-rate teachers, a large playground, classes in art and music, and plenty of sports along with the full academic curriculum.

My father was a salesman for City Refrigerator, a small company that manufactured supermarket furniture: freezer cases, shelving, checkout stands. They supplied Vons Markets, among others, and Dad was said to be honest and smart.

A strapping farm boy from Indiana (some thought he looked a bit like Clark Gable), Dad was doing well at Indiana University when a football leg injury stopped him cold. The bone became infected, and after unsuccessful treatment Dad moved to California "to die," he said.

In Los Angeles Dad met Ernest Holmes, the founder of the Church of Religious Science. They became friends, and Dad credited Holmes, a gifted metaphysician, with spiritually healing his damaged leg.

Around the same time, Dad met Elsa, my mother. She drove into a gas station where he was the attendant. He flashed a smile (great teeth). She gasped. Both were beautiful. Both, for better or worse, fell in love right there at the gas pump.

The handsome young couple, Elsa and Chuck, visited my mother's parents' home several times, and Grandpa was polite to the new boyfriend. When they announced their plans to marry, though, Grandpa vehemently told them that he did not approve of Chuck at all, and that he opposed the marriage. Perhaps he thought a farm boy was beneath his lovely daughter—or maybe he saw a flash of meanness in Chuck's eye. When the two lovebirds announced that they would wed in spite of Grandpa's opposition, though, the old man relented. He said that loving his only daughter as he did, he would, despite his objections, support their union unequivocally.

A couple of years after they married, my brother, Bill, was born. Six and a half years later I slid into the world from that unknown world of spirit, trailing, as all babies do, clouds of glory. The clouds lingered; the glory got a bit iffy.

Elsa was an excellent mother. She was lovely looking, quite talented in both music and acting, and had thought seriously of a career in the theater. Acquiescing to the mores of the day (ladies didn't have careers), she happily became a domestic slave, a housewife. She shopped and cooked (very well), she cleaned and laundered and ironed (perfect shirts). She kept the accounts and paid the bills. She helped with our homework and worried about our grades. She cared for our ills (before vaccination was available we all got chicken pox, measles, and mumps). She was, especially in the early years, strong and funny and always available. Strangely, though, despite her awesome sense of duty, despite her talent and charm, Mom silently suffered a dearth of self-confidence, exacerbated over the years by her husband's covert suppression, and she had almost no aptitude for self-knowledge. Or so it seems to me now. But then, introspection wasn't exactly de rigueur fifty years ago.

When I was about five, Nonnie, my grandmother, came to live with us after she lost her husband. Grandpa had unluckily walked by a pile of burning ragweed to which he was extremely allergic. He arrived home feeling rotten and took to his bed. Nonnie tucked him in and went to brew some tea. When she returned, steaming cup in hand, he was dead.

My grandparents had lived just over the hills in the San Fernando Valley before it was so haphazardly developed. It was all orange groves and walnut orchards—an agricultural wonderland in which a little kid could wander for days. I loved to visit them.

Grandpa had smoked a pipe that made their whole house smell good. In his workshop he built all sorts of exotic things from wood: model sailing ships and carved furniture and ornaments. He had been quite successful buying and selling real estate in the twenties. At one time he owned a considerable chunk of the Hollywood Hills, but, alas, he lost it all when the Depression hit. Nonnie possessed the greenest of thumbs and tended a lavish acre of flowers and fruit trees. They had black widow spiders in their garage, which we'd kill with bug spray. High adventure!

Nonnie was a welcome addition to our home. She was the only member of the family who really knew who she was. She liked herself, and she loved us. And she made great pancakes, spaghetti, and apple pie.

It's interesting that some of us are born with, or acquire along the way, a dark sea of inner doubt and insecurity that keeps us adrift, continually swimming to catch up, while others, like my grandmother, seem to charge into life with eager confidence, seldom questioning their worthiness. Nonnie was quite happy just being Nonnie.

As a kid, I idolized my older brother, Bill. At that age six years makes an enormous difference—he seemed to know and be able to do just about everything. Though an indifferent student, Bill was handsome, lively, great at sports, and often a lot of fun. He was "popular," as we used to say, and adored by the schoolgirls, who were gaga over him. I was proud to be his little brother. I couldn't understand why Mom sometimes said Bill had an "inferiority complex." To me he seemed way ahead of the pack.

Which brings us closer to the Chamberlain Family Paradox—our multiple feet of clay.

Dad was an imposing fellow, with a big voice and a room-dominating personality. From the remote heights of his mythic, self-aggrandizing authority, he ruled our household and provided for our needs. He was the majestic and mysterious source of our security, and our ultimate judge (doesn't this sound like the conventional image of God?). He somehow convinced us that his natural gifts and his accomplishments were far beyond anything we might ever attain. He was intelligent, sometimes charming, sometimes charmingly cruel, always in command, except on rare occasions when the presence of an even more august personality would cause a certain fading of his confidence. (I remember whenever Bill Wilson, the celebrated cofounder of Alcoholics Anonymous, came to visit us, Dad's overbearing presence seemed to shrivel.) Dad loved his work and was a good provider. And, for reasons of his own, he was a drunk, or more precisely, a periodic alcoholic.

Why Dad blitzed his brains with booze was a complete mystery to us at the time. Looking back, it's obvious to me that his inner sea of doubt and insecurity beneath his towering façade was darker for him than for the rest of us. Towering, domineering façades are not built by people at ease with themselves. And I remember how cool and unbending his mother was, running her small Indiana farm. She was a devout

Methodist and thought Dad was damned for his drinking, and, when he sobered up, that he was damned for turning to AA instead of her church. Dad desperately and unsuccessfully sought her approval and affection most of his life, driving his old Ford "back east" to Evansville at least once every year until she died. She never told any of her five children that she loved them.

Dad's periodic drinking—a few weeks on the wagon, a few weeks off—actually increased his enormous power over the family. Sober times brought us relative happiness and security; drunken times dashed hopes and fed anxiety. (Our glorious leader seems to have gone mad! Will we starve and be forced to beg in the streets?) None of us knew anything about alcoholism. When Dad was sober he may not have been a barrel of laughs, but we felt safe; the family would hold together. His periods of drunkenness were to his children inexplicable, insane, and dangerous.

We loved Christmas. Even with limited means, we always made a big deal out of it; we always had the biggest, prettiest tree in the neighborhood and lots of presents. Our family seemed happiest during these holidays.

One Christmas, when I was around seven, Dad was off the sauce, and it seemed like we'd be having a sober Yule: Hopes were high. After I'd gone to bed the night before Christmas Eve, I heard Dad drive into the garage, heard the car door slam, heard Mom open the back door to greet him, and heard Dad say in a guilty (or was it a bit sadistic?) little boy singsongy voice: "Honey, I'm drunk again." Mom said, "Oh, Chuck, no," and everything seemed to collapse. With four little words, Dad transformed our Christmas into a kind of soggy nightmare. That's power.

After graduating from college, my brother, Bill, made the mistake of going to work for Dad at City Refrigerator Company, where Dad was now boss. After several months with the company, Bill went to Dad's office with a detailed plan to increase efficiency on their production line. As Bill was explaining his well-thought-out plan, Dad quietly got up, put on his coat and hat, and walked out without comment or acknowledgment of any kind, leaving Bill talking to thin air. Later when a friend of the family said privately to Dad that he thought he was much too hard on Bill, Dad replied that he knew he was, but he just couldn't help it.

Shortly after Dad joined AA around 1943, my mother became very active in Al-Anon, the organization for the beleaguered families of alcoholics. She started one of the first Al-Anon groups in Beverly Hills, which often met at our home, and then formed another in Laguna Beach when they moved there in 1956. One evening Dad walked into the kitchen where Mom and I were clearing up after dinner and out of the blue began explaining to her why her work in Al-Anon was really quite trivial compared with his profound work in AA. Helping non-alcoholics was child's play, hardly worth notice compared with saving alcoholics. But when a *real* sinner like himself found God and sobriety, all the angels in heaven rejoiced!

Another time, when I was about fifteen, my newly sober dad called us all into the living room and, sitting in his big throne chair, explained that he, like Christ, might be "called" by God to abandon us and go out into the world to heal the sick with his newfound divine powers. He was dead serious, and we felt we suddenly didn't matter at all. Mom quietly wept. What a shame that we were too intimidated to see the wacky humor in his absurd fantasy; we missed a good laugh. But then again there was the fear of laughing Dad right back into his bourbon bottle. The danger of a return to booze was still a veiled threat, an effective way to control us. As luck would have it, though, the "call" never came, and Dad stayed home.

I remember, in later years, visiting my folks shortly after returning from a life-changing seventeen-day spiritual workshop. I was excited and inspired by my first glimpse of openheartedness, and the wonderful experience of meditation. Ever the optimist, I thought Dad would be delighted to hear about these discoveries. After I'd finished sharing my experience with him, his only comment was that if you look like you're meditating, you're not meditating. In our family code he was saying: For great mystics like him, all of life is a meditation; they don't have to sit in silence with their eyes closed like us poseurs.

Dad was never physically violent; he never hit us or pushed us around. His violence was psychological. When he was drunk, he'd stagger recklessly around the house or slump in his big living room chair, emitting angry vibes that seemed to me like a radiance of pure evil. It was like living with the devil. And he could quell anything remotely like fun and frolic with his famously lethal sneer. That sneer was like being slashed with a machete.

I think Mom suffered the most. Dad's drinking drove her into a deep despair that, try as she might, she couldn't hide from her kids.

And there were unpredictable episodes of genuine insanity, the drunkard's terror: delirium tremens. Dad would have horrifying hallucinations of being savagely attacked by rats, or feeling that his face and body and bed and the whole room were covered with scurrying cockroaches. Off and on, we were living with a madman. I don't know how he managed to keep working at City Refrigerator; I guess he was just too good at the market business to get fired.

When I was about nine years old, the booze had beat up Dad so badly that he finally "hit bottom." One night Mom, Nonnie, and I were playing cards in the living room. Dad, who had been on a bender for weeks, staggered down the hall to the kitchen. We figured he was after something to eat. Suddenly there was a terrible crash of breaking dishes, and indescribable sounds issued from his fallen body.

We all ran to the kitchen. There was big, scary Dad, writhing on the floor in grotesque convulsions. We were terrified and helpless. What do you do with a flailing, slobbering body on a kitchen floor? Mom managed to call for an ambulance. They came quickly and carted Dad away. We thought he might be dying.

Dad recovered, knowing he had totally lost his battle with alcohol. This colossally arrogant man at last gave up and turned to AA for help.

So there we were. My father, though holding down his job and dominating his family, was self-absorbed, lost with his demons and addiction. My mother, though a dutiful wife and mother, was unable to shield either herself or her children from her husband's covert cruelties. My brother, though athletic and glamorous, was uncertain of his aptitudes. And then there was me. Though playful and imaginative, I bobbed between unconvincing self-aggrandizement and debilitating self-doubt. We were a profusion of contradiction: four healthy, good-looking, well-educated, variously talented, well-liked people plagued by severe inner discomfort while pretending to be absolutely perfect. The Chamberlain Magic Show.

Contrary to my pretended perfection, most of my life has been ruled in one way or another by fear. Not so much by fear of outer threats like muggings or financial ruin, but by my fear of inner poverty, unworthiness, inadequacy, and especially the fear of not being fully alive, of not fitting in at all. At times I felt that God's assembly line carelessly forgot to include parts of my heart and soul. For reasons I've never understood, children of alcoholics often feel these lacks in varying degrees. A psychologist would call this warped sense of self "subjective phobia." My most frightening nemesis was none other than *me*.

If I were to look for a central dynamic in my life, it would be the long peregrination from fear to love. But I was afraid of love, afraid that love would find me unworthy, inadequate, boring. I was afraid of what I most desperately sought: to belong to humanity; to love and be loved.

So what to do?

My initial and almost lifelong response to this dilemma was to bury as deeply as possible my offending self and create an image that would be lovable, or at least likable. This process of course begins with assessing what people around me like and then trying to be those things.

Thus my life as an actor began very early. I learned to write my role and act my life. My motto was: *Please the crowd at all costs.*

And unbeknownst to me the costs were very high. A life of pretense is exhausting and debilitating. One's inner reality will eventually push through any outward show, however charming. If not, a failure to deal with one's inner turmoil and self-rejection can lead to illness, even death.

Though I've never been sure of the sources of my alienation, which began long before the revelations of puberty, I suspect it was exacerbated not only by my father's suppressive nature, but also by my being forced by family and state to enter public grammar school. I feared and loathed school. It was a traumatic loss of my former freedom. I hated being told what to do. As a four-year-old I could roam our neighborhood as I pleased finding adventure all over the place, unencumbered by responsibilities of any kind. Why, on turning five, was I thrust into the clutches of all those ornery teachers ordering me around?

My mother had to drag me kicking and tearfully protesting into the unfamiliar and terrifying cage of kindergarten. Apart from one or two other loudly defiant children being pushed in by their moms, most of the kids seemed just fine, inexplicably happy to be embarking on this big adventure. I was not mollified.

The demands of kindergarten weren't daunting, the curriculum being mostly playtime and naps, so as the days ground by I calmed down and adjusted somewhat. But I never discovered the knack of joining these confident mainstream kids who seemed to be having such a good time. For instance, the play room was equipped with large, hollow wooden blocks with which the other five-year-olds built ships or trains that you could actually get into and play conductor and such. I wasn't ever enlisted as a builder or even a passenger, so I constructed a sort of ticket office and demanded that all passengers pretend to buy a boarding ticket from me. My scam worked the first day and I was delighted with my power, but then tickets became passé and my office was dismantled to build a caboose.

Luckily in almost all situations misfits can find other misfits to commiserate and play with, and some of us strays became pals. I graduated from kindergarten without honors, but with some fun and friends.

Entering first grade was an entirely different saga. It seemed to me that our childhood idyll was instantly smashed against the rocks of adulthood, devoured by the ferocious three-headed dragon terrifyingly named Reading, Writing, and Arithmetic.

My parents had accepted the then-conventional wisdom that they should *not* interfere with schoolteachers' methods by introducing their children to any of these reptilian subjects ahead of time—I entered the dragon's den totally unprepared. While the other kids all knew that a certain three letters spelled *cat* and that two plus three equaled five, I could not for the life of me figure out what was going on.

This school stuff is definitely *not* for happy-go-lucky me, I thought, so I plunged into full-scale passive resistance. I refused to learn (while pretending to try), and I refused to play team sports. Although this passive-aggressive behavior gave me a neurotic sense of power (the power to frustrate grown-ups I seemed to have no chance of pleasing), it also made me look and feel like a real dummy. It took me ages to learn to read, for instance. Being made to stand before the class and attempt to read aloud was the sheerest agony, especially when our tall, straight-backed, gray-haired, infinitely authoritative school principal, Mrs. Abbey, was monitoring us. Math too continued to baffle me for a long while. And though I had unconsciously brought these failures on myself, at least in part, I began to feel supremely stupid and alienated from the system and from the rest of the kids, most of whom were doing very well, whizzing through those flash cards and batting those baseballs.

Dickie Venamen, who lived just across our back alley, and Arden Phillips, who lived just across the street, were my closest pals since before I can remember. Arden's family was especially dramatic. Her handsome elder brother was bedridden with undulant fever, which he caught, the doctors guessed, from drinking unpasteurized milk. But he had a very sexy girlfriend who used to spend a lot of time in his bedroom. One evening Arden's father, several sheets to the wind, kicked their pet kitten clear across their front yard. I never forgave him for that. Her mom sang in the local church choir with my mother and brother. Mom and Mrs. Phillips vied for the solo parts with smiles and covert enmity.

When I was about to enter the third grade, Dickie's industrious father invented salt and pepper shakers that released their tasty contents from the bottom when a button was pressed at the top—no more arduous shaking required. These ingenious devices quickly appeared in homes and restaurants everywhere, making the previously impoverished Venamens rich. They packed up and moved away to a mansion up in the hills with a pool table and a pinball machine. Of course they pulled Dickie out of Beverly Vista and plunked him into a posh grammar school on the right side of Wilshire Boulevard. I was dumbfounded and heartsick at the loss of my first best friend.

Dickie was a year ahead of me in school and shortly before he abandoned our neighborhood he warned me that Mrs. Redpath, the infamous third-grade teacher, actually ate children alive, a grim fate he had barely escaped. I was appropriately terrified and begged my parents not to force me into her murderous clutches. Amazingly, they ignored my fears and on the appointed day sent me off to my imminent death. For three days I pretended to go to school, but instead I just wandered around town, occasionally peeking into the playground and wondering why none of the kids were dripping blood.

The evening of the third day the school authorities called my mother wondering where I was and thus revealed my criminal truancy. I was duly lambasted, and the next morning Mom dragged me once again into the dragon's den.

As it turned out, Mrs. Redpath was a wonderful teacher. She even gave me my first starring role in a lavish student production of *The Pied Piper of Hamelin*. Decades later when I was playing Cyrano de Bergerac at the Ahmanson Theatre in Los Angeles, Mrs. Redpath, whom I hadn't seen since school, surprised me with a backstage visit after the show. It was a joy to see her again and to have the opportunity to thank her for inaugurating my acting career.

Though I missed my playmate Dickie a lot, I still had Arden—or so I thought. To my dismay, that same year the Phillips family mysteriously moved away, too, and I was doubly devastated. But Skeeter McComber and Mousie Newman were still around and somehow I got over it. Besides, we had a real gangster in the neighborhood to contend with.

Tony Carnero, a former bootlegger and current gambling czar, lived in a modest house next to ours. He was a stocky fellow of medium height with black, slicked-back hair and ebony eyes. He always dressed in a dark suit and hat and had the potent look and romantic aura of the movie mobster. Carnero was one of the powers behind the *Lux*, a large ship he'd converted into a spectacular gambling casino that was anchored three miles off the California coast beyond the reach of the law. To the consternation of the authorities, gamblers were transported back and forth in luxurious motor launches that the police were powerless to stop. The Lux was a smashing success and a thorn in the paws of the cops and politicos alike.

Carnero's house was protected by an elaborate electronic eye mechanism that surrounded his property. This fascinated all of us kids, and we occasionally dared to try to set off the alarm, but without success. I guess it was turned on only late at night.

Once in a while when I was little, and things weren't going my way, I used to go down to the bottom of the low hedge that separated our two houses and yell and cry as loud as I could, alerting the entire neighborhood to my woe. Carnero, tired of my infantile operas, came outside during one of these tirades and, instead of threatening to take out a contract on me, said quite sweetly that if I cut out the noise for good he would give me an "A Number 1" Christmas present every year. I shut up, and Tony gave me a nifty little red bicycle on Christmas.

Earl Warren, the governor of California, was mighty unhappy to have Carnero's Lux operating so blatantly off his coast. The governor's investigators finally discovered two helpful facts. They found an obscure old law on the books that forbade ships without engines from mooring in California waters, and they discovered that the Lux had no engine. They were able to raid and close down the floating casino, thus handing Earl Warren a "great" victory and paving his way to the United States Supreme Court, where he became a remarkable Chief Justice.

Carnero then became involved in building the Stardust Hotel and Casino in Las Vegas where the waters seemed more welcoming. However, there were apparently dangerous behind-the-scenes power plays even in gambling-friendly Vegas.

One summer evening our family was having dinner in the breakfast room, which faced Carnero's house. It was hot and Dad was sitting at the head of a small table in his undershirt, showing lots of chest hair. He was sober, the pot roast was tasty, and all was well until we heard a single gunshot that seemed to come from Tony's house. My brother and I sprang up to run outside and see what was happening, at which point Dad said with absolute command, "Sit right back down, boys! There aren't going to be any witnesses from *this* house." We heard an ambulance siren coming fast. It stopped at Tony's briefly and then wailed off to the hospital. Soon the police came to question us. Dad told them that we had heard the shot at about 6:20 P.M., but that we had seen nothing. The cops left disappointed.

About half an hour later, Barbara, Tony's live-in girlfriend, came to our door all disheveled and sobbing, begging us to let her stay with us for a few days because she was terrified to stay at home. After she had calmed down a little, she told us that Tony had been shot. A deliveryman had come with a package for Mr. Carnero. Barbara had answered the door and called for Tony. When Tony came to the door, the delivery guy, whose hand was surreptitiously inside the package with a hidden gun, shot Tony in the stomach, ran to his nondescript car at the curb, and zoomed off like a rocket.

With her bleached hair and a certain female swagger, Barbara wasn't the classiest gal in town, but we'd found her friendly and rather sweet underneath her tough-dolly veneer. Of course Mom asked her to stay with us. She slept in Bill's bed in the small bedroom he and I shared, and Bill moved to the living room couch. That evening Barbara seemed to fall asleep instantly, but all through the night I heard her quietly weeping.

The next morning I wolfed down my breakfast and ran off to school to achieve at least temporary celebrity by regaling my newly admiring fellow students with wild tales of gangland warfare right next door. To my everlasting dismay, Mousie Newman's brother, Kurt, who lived across the street and was my neighborhood nemesis, had already told the story a dozen times on the playground, achieving stardom and making me last year's headlines. My celebrity would have to wait a couple more decades.

Two days later, Barbara asked me to take the suit that Tony was shot in to the dry cleaners—I got to see the bloody bullet hole and everything. My school chums were still unimpressed. Kurt remained the Mario Puzo of Beverly Vista School.

Carnero survived the shooting, but about a year later he mysteriously died at the Stardust Hotel. His shady cronies claimed it was a heart attack, but Dad was pretty sure they'd decided to snuff him for good. As usual, high drama in the neighborhood often superseded the subtler difficulties lurking beneath the surface at home and at school.

Abandoned by my friends Dickie and Arden and with adolescence approaching, I was troubled by another potentially disastrous problem. I began to notice that I was more attracted sexually to boys than to girls. In high school I played the game and had several wonderful girlfriends. We'd go to dances and neck in the backseats of friends' cars like everybody else (I was known as a great kisser), but it grew ever more clear to me that my heart was elsewhere.

At the beginning of this new millennium when our understanding of homosexuality is slowly leading to acceptance and, better yet, disinterest, it's difficult for those who weren't around in the forties and fifties to appreciate how deeply terrifying it was to imagine being labeled a faggot, a pansy, a pervert. It seemed to me then that even traitors and murderers were generally held in higher esteem than I would be if anyone ever found out the truth about me. I remember walking home from school one day solemnly swearing to myself over and over that I would never ever reveal my loathsome secret in any way to anyone.

This solemn commitment to deception reminds me of the most purely honest thing I've ever done, perhaps my last absolutely honest and independent act for decades. It happened during an eighth-grade YMCA track meet. I could always run faster than everyone else in grammar school, and I'd never been beaten in a race. The YMCA meet involved several grammar schools and took place at the Beverly Hills High School track. I was scheduled to run in the hundred-yard dash.

The starting gun was fired and we all took off. To my great surprise I noticed a kid from another school pulling out ahead of me so I put on more speed. So did he. Try as I might, I couldn't catch up with him. So I just quit running and walked off the track. I had no interest in running a race that I couldn't win. What was the point?

My father (sober) was there on the field, and he ran over to me with several of my school friends wanting to know if I'd pulled a muscle or something. I said no, I just wasn't winning so why bother. To my utter amazement they all were scandalized. What about sportsmanship? What about team spirit! Shame! The disapproval of one's tribe is potent indeed. Win or lose, I've never stopped in the middle of a race again, but I still feel that what I did that day was totally fresh and free and honest, and delightfully oblivious of the dreaded norm.

An alcoholic father, scholastic paralysis, and sexual dismay certainly aggravated my self-esteem problem, but I suspect I may have entered life with this particular challenge of imagined worthlessness, which by the way would eventually push me to a long, sometimes bumpy journey toward self-discovery and healing—toward love. Sometimes the intense discomfort of that irritating grain of sand creates a pearl. Fortunately, along with the pain and fear inherent to this progress, I had a nascent interest in spiritual possibilities and an irrational sense that somehow I would someday make a big splash in life.

Interlacing these stormy times were rays of sunshine. As a youngster at home I had a warm relationship with my mother and superb grandmother. Between fights, Bill and I had fine times.

In these early years, Mom was funny, athletic, and playful. An actress and a stage director in college and at the Ebell Theatre in Los Angeles, and an excellent pianist and singer from a musical family, Mom was always an interested audience for my juvenile playlets and piano lessons. We used to love to whistle tunes in harmony while washing dishes and doing other chores. And Mom did a great orangutan imitation.

When I was small, Nonnie used to wake me at dawn to watch the colors of the sunrise. After dinner she'd sometimes take me for a long walk in the neighborhood. As we strolled, we both liked to peer into people's front windows from the sidewalk to get a glimpse of how they lived. Nonnie was as close to a raconteur as a woman could get in those days. She'd tell endless stories about how her family crossed from Nebraska to California in covered wagons, about their scary adventures with the Indians, about her sister Ella, who was the first white woman ever to climb to the top of Mount Whitney, and about her brief, but colorful career as a professional singer. Nonnie had one of those "Star Is Born" experiences in *The Merry Widow* on Broadway just after the turn of the century. She had a small part in the operetta and because of her wonderful voice she was understudy to the star. Well, on opening night the star fell ill and Nonnie went on in the lead and brought the house down. The next day she got marvelous reviews, but after a few weeks she quit the show and returned home, saying she just didn't like show business—too much backbiting, she said.

Six and a half years older than me, my brother, Bill, won all our fights, but he was at times great fun. He carried me around on his shoulders and played all sorts of games—once in a while he let me ride his racing bike. And I was fascinated by his numerous girlfriends, all top-of-the-line gorgeous and the most sought after in school.

In high school and college I always had a group of close friends and lots of interesting activities. Even neurotics can enjoy good times, though the unreality and pretense at the center of neurosis increasingly demand one's attention.

Following my mediocre performance in high school I was happily surprised to be accepted by Pomona College, a highly respected institution in Claremont, California. Though my high school grades had been average at best, I scored high on the SAT tests, and I had an interesting list of extracurricular activities. I'd been a four-year letterman in track, chief justice of the Student Court (not a friend-winning position), and I'd won an art department award and a summer scholarship to Art Center School. Much to my surprise I'd also been voted most reserved, most sophisticated, and best physique by our Beverly Hills High senior yearbook staff, a trio of accolades bound to impress the most dour of admissions officers.

In 1952 Pomona was one of three small colleges nestled among the fragrant orange groves of a then sparsely developed agricultural area of Los Angeles County, at the foot of snowy peaked Mount Baldy. Coed Pomona, Scripts College, and Claremont Men's College were all adjacent to the sleepy little town of Claremont with its single cinema and ever-popular hamburger joint.

The campuses of both Scripts and Pomona were idyllically beautiful, with classically designed, vine-covered buildings surrounded by towering sycamores, California oaks, and lovely parks and fountains. Pomona secretly thought of itself as "the Oxford of the Orange Belt."

An old-fashioned liberal arts college, Pomona had high scholastic standards, and the leisurely, romantic aura that graced such institutions before the glories of art and literature and philosophy were overrun by the clamor of technology and commerce. This was the perfect place for a dreamy romantic to discover the riches of human thought and creativity, removed from the harshness, insecurities, and competitive scrambles that all students face after graduation.

Even with my lousy work habits, emotional confusion, and general unease, I was dazzled by Pomona's rich curriculum. I could have imagined no future more wonderful than the glamour of acting, but my near catatonic inhibition and terror of appearing ridiculous led me to the even less practical choice of majoring in painting and art history. Practicality was nowhere to be found in my nature—I somehow figured that if I couldn't make it as an actor, I *could* support myself as a painter, perhaps a commercial artist.

Partly because I lived on campus, tuition was considerably higher than my folks could afford. My grandmother had given my mother stock in a previously defunct oil well in Lodi, California, and in what seemed like intervention from on high, this considerate well began to produce precious black crude just as we were making plans for Pomona. It continued to produce for four years. My mother's share paid for my higher education and then the well went dry as mysteriously as it had become unexpectedly wet. My undying thanks go to Mom *and* to Mother Nature!

I loved learning to paint and sculpt, and my art history professors were fascinating. But early in my freshman year I made the mistake of joining some new friends at Pomona's legendary Holmes Hall Theatre to watch tryouts for a college play, a deathless comedy called *George Washington Slept Here*. The director, Virginia Allen, spotted me in the audience and persuaded me, against my ardent objections, to read for the part of the flamboyant actor. I did get up and read a scene, undoubtedly very badly, and for enigmatic reasons Mrs. Allen gave me the part.

This was the beginning of Richard the art major moonlighting as a perennial DP. DP was the current, slightly unkind acronym referring to members of Drama Productions. It also had overtones of Displaced Persons. Despite my shyness and inexperience, I got a few laughs as the egocentric actor and I was hooked.

In the early 1950s the Korean War was still recent history and young men were subject to the draft. I had a college deferment and had to maintain a B average to stay in school. Because I was spending so much unaccredited time in drama department activities, and still more time as a member of Pomona's track team (running the hundred-yard dash, the two-twenty, and the four-forty relay), I started to have trouble earning decent grades in my official studies. So I managed to avoid as many difficult courses as I could; when it was possible to take the likes of music appreciation instead of physics or a foreign language, I did so.

Though I was fast losing my heart to drama, I didn't switch majors because as a performer I was still desperately inhibited by self-doubt. I had to rehearse on my own *before* play rehearsals because I was afraid to try anything new in real rehearsals that I hadn't carefully planned out beforehand. I did not trust myself to find my character spontaneously with the other actors. Acting during these years (and to some extent even later on) was an anxious mix of elation and terror.

It wasn't until my senior year that I had a life-changing breakthrough as a neophyte actor. I'd been in many plays the past three years and must have improved because Mrs. Allen cast me as Bluntchly in Bernard Shaw's *Arms and the Man*. Like his name, Bluntchly was straightforward, wry, practical, and very funny, and in the end he even got the girl. I loved this character and worked very hard on the part, but I didn't manage to break loose into an all-stops-out performance until opening night. Somehow the audience brought me fully alive, and I managed to give a really spirited performance (in amateur terms) and pretty much stole the show. When I made my final exit following a brilliantly written speech, the audience broke into thunderous applause that stopped the show cold. Holmes Hall was filled with laughter and cheering for all four performances, and I was delirious with the joyous realization that maybe I *could* embrace my first love and actually become an actor! I gleefully decided to throw fine arts out the window and give my heart unreservedly to acting, that great escape.

By the time I graduated from college I'd figured out how to live (well, get by) in the protective, richly diverse world of academia. Now, like all former students, I'd have to figure out how to live in that huge, raucous, foreign-looking Real World out there.

So how did this hopeful but inwardly lost product of the Chamberlain Magic Show, well trained in covering intense insecurity with the pretense of outward "perfection," plan to cope with his long-delayed debut into Real Life?

My strategy, only partly conscious, was to continue the construction and maintenance of my self-image—the alternate, much improved Richard I presented to the world—to refine my ability as a pleaser, and to strive with all my might toward that big splash which would justify my existence on the planet. Not a healthy mix.

ON MAKING
A BIG SPLASH

There are worlds of difference between the "humble nobody" who may achieve great things but cares nothing for prestige, and the "neurotic nobody" for whom prestige is *everything*, his lifeblood. As a near perfect neurotic nobody I was desperate to at least *seem* to belong, so I became obsessed with somehow making the big splash that would catapult me up the hierarchical ladder to "somebodyhood."

Shortly before graduating from Pomona College in 1956, I was approached by a talent scout from Paramount Studios who had seen me in a couple of college plays. She wanted to set up a meeting for me with some studio executives who might want to put me under contract. I was flabbergasted.

Bachelor of arts degree in hand, I *did* meet with these studio suits, and they *did* offer a seven-year contract. I sought advice from a family friend on the fringe of show biz and proceeded to attempt to negotiate terms with Paramount on my own, not being able to afford a lawyer.

The executives, who no doubt had chewed up and spit out plenty of performers and agents with real savvy, must have found my puny attempts at negotiating a fair salary hilarious. Mercifully I was saved from signing myself into slavery by the dreaded draft notice. I toppled from my fanciful dreams of fame and fortune into the very real drudgery of enlisted army life.

The U.S. Army and I were not exactly made for each other—mine is not a militant nature. If I felt an alien in civilian life, I was positively Andromedan in the infantry.

My basic training took place at Fort Ord in northern California. If kindergarten had seemed like intolerable bondage, then basic was the beginning of a life sentence at Sing Sing without parole. There were two bright spots. The first was a hot competition between the various company mess halls for the best wall mural. Our company commander noticed that I'd been an art major and drafted me to paint our mess hall mural in whatever spare time I could find. He wanted a vast picture of San Francisco's famous Fisherman's Wharf, eighteen by thirty feet. So I painted while everybody else ate. We all thought the mural turned out really well, but about a week after I'd finished, the new general in charge of the whole fort issued orders stating that murals were immoral and unmanly. He demanded that they be painted over with standard hospital green. Never mind, I had fun painting the thing.

A logistical glitch of some kind created the second bright spot—we were allowed, in fact ordered, to go home for a two-week break at Christmas (I'd been inducted in early December).

It was shortly after this blissful, unexpected break that I wrote the following letter to my best friend in college, Joe:

Dear Joe,

If you're an observant ex-Marine, you've noticed that it's Sunday. Your old pal has toted his stationery into the hilly, mossy woods overlooking Monterey Bay. Tiny white lines of sea foam appear and disappear far below along the coast, while a martyred sky supports tons of pompous Roman clouds. The neighborhood dogs bark in intermittent conversation (which, feeling left out, I try unsuccessfully to join). Amplified church bells drone flaccid Presbyterian melodies, and an early spring already begins to stab the earth with wee green hints of tomorrow's underbrush. This should be enough, but I guess we're pretty hard to please.

And about that letter from Nan extolling the arts! Christ, I've wasted so much time fearing the arts were a refuge for the gutless—how nice to be disillusioned.

Would you know what I mean when I say that I've learned from the army that to live well is not so complicated and difficult a matter as I once imagined? Within this drudgery, simple things mean a lot.

And have you felt the disappointment in this military predicament of speaking to an intelligent face and receiving a sort of grunting reply? Some of these guys are made of good stuff, but just don't know what to do with it.

Don't remember telling you much about my Christmas leave. One evening just before The Birthday I was home alone at my folks' house in Laguna Beach, sipping wine and writing letters. Handel's Messiah *suddenly plunged forth from the radio, and since we of the Pomona College choir sang this work Christmas before last, it brought forth such painful nostalgia for all those wonderful times that I listened and cried shamelessly for about half an hour.*

Needless to say this made me realize I had a lot of unfinished business to attend to so I decided to make a private safari back to the old campus and stroll about packing away the treasured past for good so that I might proceed into the future (i.e., the army) with something more like composure. Well I did, and it worked.

Cheers,
Rich

After basic training at Fort Ord, I was sent to Korea and made company clerk of the infantry company. The job may sound like easy pickings, but it was in fact complex and quite difficult, and it saved my sanity. I plunged into my work with concentration I'd never known before. Work helped me escape from the colossal boredom of regimented life in the middle of nowhere (after the Korean War, South Korea was, though naturally beautiful, devastated).

During my entire sixteen-month tour I was allowed only one R&R to Japan, but I made the most of that fabulous week. Here's a portion of another letter I wrote at the time to Joe:

> *I've caught up with you, Joseph. I am a MAN (as of 0230, 8 Dec. 57), and I characterize the experience not as dramatic or monumental or artistic, but simply as enormously pleasant. Following a two-day flirtation, this enchanting creature and I proceeded, partially plastered, to an ancient Japanese hotel of her choice, immersed ourselves in a pool of fragrant, steaming water, donned flowing kimonos, floated up a narrow flight of shiny wooden stairs worn smooth by centuries of shoeless feet, and plopped into bed. It was all so charmingly easy, so utterly enjoyable. Then to be awakened the following dawn with sandy-eyed tenderness, sober, to enjoy lengthily our lazy warmth. This comprises my sole memory of Japan.*

There was, I admit, another avenue of escape. After several months I finally made some friends and after work we used to drink ourselves into oblivion almost every night at the Enlisted Men's club, where a bottle of beer cost a quarter. Once in a while we'd get a weekend pass to go into Seoul. Here's part of a letter I wrote to Joe about these jaunts into the capital city:

> *Take Miss Pearl S. Buck, add a dash of shattered plate glass, and blend in a liberal amount of Coca-Cola to the rhythm of ancient auto horns, bicycle bells, and clomping oxen, and you'll end up with an inedible concoction called Seoul. The accidental beauty of makeshift, primitive constructions, brown bodies draped in flashing white cloth, the fresh green of vegetable patches inter-*

rupting filthy grays. Glance through an open shutter into a room just large enough to contain the bed that supports a flat-faced, thickly painted prostitute applying more paint. It's early morning, by the way, and sunlight is just beginning to break itself against lines of locust trees, shattering down among dust, bamboo, and mounds of old rubber tires, filtering through streams of charcoal smoke—the residue of millions of bitty breakfast fires.

Silent faces drift into the street and perch upon squatting bodies that have been there behind apple baskets and turnips for centuries. Bare lightbulbs still burn in showcases full of Korean candies, American watches, and various cures for clap. (It should be warned that said cures are not too reliable. Upon awakening one morning and finding himself alarmingly puffed up, a buddy of mine queried the local medic concerning his condition only to discover that the shot of penicillin he had recently received from a clandestine Korean "physician" was actually Wild Root Cream Oil hair tonic). Everybody sells and nobody buys. I guess they end up eating their own damned apples. And where these apples come from is not lesser among Asian mysteries. There are no apple trees in Korea.

With the sun come the Slicky-Boys and of course their sisters in iniquity. Slicky-Boys are thoroughly charming youngsters, expert in everything from vulgar theft to the fine art of pimpery. They'll pimp for their sisters and mothers, and even for their fathers if you happen to be so disposed.

Children outside the city are far less needy and therefore far less wicked. Last Sunday a friend and I were out in the country on a camera tour when we ran across two little fellows fooling around on the dirt road. We quickly made friends and raced and piggy-backed etc. for quite a ways. Friend and I were going to buy the poor skinny little creatures something to eat, but they would have none of it—they wanted us to eat with them and their family at their nearby bamboo cottage. We would have too, but GIs aren't

*allowed to associate with the villagers. Too bad. We missed out on
something really interesting.*

My compulsively hard work at company headquarters made me
indispensable, and my captain promoted me to the rank of staff sergeant. This gave me entrée into our camp's real bar, and, with the hard
stuff, quicker inebriation.

After two years of this curious routine of hard work and booze
(being the son of an alcoholic I did begin to worry a bit about the lat-
ter), I was honorably and happily discharged and sent home with a
much-improved work ethic and a few hundred dollars saved from my
lavish army pay.

My new freedom was a joy, but my prospects for "the big splash"
seemed bleak. My friend Joe tried to talk me into trying my luck in
New York, where he was breaking into musical theater, but somehow I
felt compelled to pursue my destiny in Los Angeles. *"Now I do want to
'make it' in the East, and I don't much like the West, and I do want to get
far away from home sweet home, but I am totally committed to a life or
death tussle here. And it is a beauteous thing finally to be committed,"* I
wrote Joe on my father's stationery, just after being discharged from
the army. For a few uncomfortable months I lived with my parents in
their new home on Bayview Place in Laguna Beach. I stayed downstairs next to the garage in a small room filled with the same bedroom
furniture I grew up with in the Beverly Hills house. Eerie. After about
six weeks of feeling slightly unwelcome in my folks' house, I went
downstairs to bed one night and had a very spooky surprise. Instead of
sliding into bed as usual, for some mysterious reason I flung back the
covers and was stunned to find a large, lively scorpion quite alert and
poised to strike standing right smack in the middle of the mattress.
The poisonous insect was positioned so perfectly that it seemed to
have been carefully placed. If there was a message in all this I got it. As
soon as I could I bought the cheapest car I could find with my army

dough and found a tiny apartment in L.A. around Western and Santa Monica Boulevards right next to the Hollywood Freeway. At sixty bucks a month it was noisy and smoggy, the neighborhood was depressing and sort of scary, my fellow tenants were mostly ancient and nearing death, the kitchen had bugs, the bed was a sagging contraption you pulled down from a wall, and I loved the place! It was a minifortress from which I'd one way or another storm the gates of Hollywood. And no scorpions!

During my two years of exile in Korea most of my college friends had scattered across the country to seek their fortunes. One pal from those idyllic ivory-tower days, Bob Towne, *did* answer the old phone number I called and we got together to catch up.

I'd always been somewhat in awe of Bob. Women found him exciting, and his love life was the stuff of legend even before graduation. He was a serious and talented writer, a bright student, and a good actor to boot. We had acted together in several college plays, including *The Crucible* and the aforementioned production of *Arms and the Man,* in which he played Sergius to my Bluntschli. (In the early seventies I wasn't surprised when Bob caused a sensation by writing the screenplay for *Chinatown,* Roman Polanski's brilliant film noir about the Los Angeles we had grown up in. Years later he wrote something about screenwriting that struck me as just right. Never underestimate the suggestions of an actor when rewriting a script, because the actor, if he or she is any good, will almost invariably get deeper into his or her character than the writer has. The actor's insights can be extremely useful.)

Bob said he was planning to audition for the hottest actors' workshop in town taught by Jeff Corey (a disciple of the Method) and suggested that I try out, too. With considerable trepidation I made an appointment to meet Corey in the garage studio behind his Hollywood home. On the appointed day I approached him with shaky knees and luckily was bidden to sit.

Jeff Corey had been blacklisted in the 1950s after being called in front of the House Un-American Activities Committee. He refused to name names. For twelve years he couldn't get an acting job, so he turned his considerable talents to teaching. Among his many students were Kirk Douglas, Anthony Perkins, Jack Nicholson, Barbra Streisand, and, briefly, James Dean. Jeff's appearance—craggy features, bushy eyebrows, and the intense gaze of a Tolkien wizard—was formidable. I was equally fascinated and terrified. I worked up all the charm I could muster, called forth my old game of appearing intelligent, and tried to exhibit some sort of potential.

It worked! Jeff accepted me in his beginners group. I was overjoyed. As I was leaving he said, "You're very formal, aren't you?" I said that I hadn't really thought about it, but, yes, I guess I was. He replied, "That's an interesting way to stay safe." If I were to characterize in its simplest form our work together for the next two years, I'd say it was the struggle between his challenge to risk and be free and my fearful need for what I thought was the safety of my all-American boy image.

Bob was accepted, too. We arrived early the evening of our first class, walked along the driveway to the backyard, and sat on the lawn with the other new students, trying to look cool as we waited for Jeff Corey to emerge from his house and open up the studio. Bob and I were excited and very nervous, wondering if we were falling into the ferocious clutches of a West Coast Lee Strasberg. In due time Jeff did appear and invited us into his studio. And so it began.

One of the first things Jeff said was that the theater is a temple—whenever you enter it, wear shoes. He meant that, possible fame and fortune aside, acting is a deeply serious and sometimes profound art, and that we must approach our training with the utmost respect. With Jeff as our teacher it was hard not to.

Our work in class focused mainly on improvisation and scene work. The improvisations began with Jeff calling two or three students onstage and describing a basic dramatic situation, for instance a couple on the verge of divorce. Then Jeff would whisper to each actor his or her foremost action or desire in the scene. He might whisper to the girl that in her view her husband is ruining her life, stifling her, and that she must get rid of him as quickly as possible in order to rejoin her secret lover. Then he might whisper to the fellow that he loves his wife more than life itself and must convince her to stay with him and rekindle their love or die trying. The actors then improvise this drama using their imaginations and hopefully tapping into their personal emotions, experience, and power.

Some of the students became very good at involving themselves emotionally in these improvs. My problem was that I had long ago rejected my real self (whoever that might be—I didn't want to know) and presented to the world (and to myself) a remarkably perfect Richard. My real feelings were unavailable to me and unwelcome. So I had to think fast and fake it most of the time. I had a creative imagination and I improvised reasonably well on occasion, but you can't fool all the people all the time, and Jeff was always on my case to get real. It took years of therapy and various consciousness workshops to accomplish that. So I was in the complex position of having to improvise not as myself (which was the whole point), but as the character Perfect Richard that I was already playing full-time in life. I was the "bad" me pretending to be the "good" me who was then improvising or acting a character in scene work. No wonder I was tired all the time.

Most of my friends those days came from Jeff's classes—excited, ambitious, lively young hopefuls. And, wonder of wonders, in this heady new atmosphere of artistic discovery, I fell in love for the first time in my uptight life. Of course I'd had secret crushes before, but this was the first time all those falling-in-love mechanisms Mother Nature so exuberantly built into our minds and bodies were powerful enough to mow down my titanic shame and fear.

On our first date Dave took me to his favorite restaurant, the Golden Pagoda, in L.A.'s Chinatown. The romantic vibes of new love made it seem like Shangri-la. Just going to the movies or cooking up some dinner or hiking in the mountains was wonderful fun in the swirl of first romance. Our idyll lasted about a year and was pure delight. This was the simplest, most trouble-free relationship I've ever had, which is amazing considering how inhibited I'd been previously, and how emotionally confused I remained afterward. Prejudice was still rampant in the late 1950s so we kept our affair as secret as possible, even from our friends. I think my experience of unexpected freedom during this clandestine interlude was made possible by my friend's conta-giously easy, playful nature and by the fact that I was as yet unknown and therefore blissfully anonymous. Eventually a fellow student caught Dave's eye, and we were back to being "just friends." The separation hurt, but fickle youth recovers quickly.

Very few of us were finding much work, so we formed our own the-ater group called The Angel's Company and put on a number of well-received plays like *La Ronde* and *The Caine Mutiny Court-Martial.* I was taking singing and dancing lessons as well and was getting a rep for hard work and discipline (as opposed to the wild and risky freedom coming into fashion at the time).

A family friend introduced me to an agent named Lilly Messinger. Lilly was a small, stout woman but quite grand. She had been Louis B. Mayer's assistant during the glory days of MGM, was married to a mys-terious prince, and was officially known as Princess Lilly Turntaxis. She was a friend of Marlene Dietrich, and Joan Crawford had once lived in her guesthouse (the windows of which were rigged, for reasons never explained, with pipes to produce the appearance of rain). I wrote to Joe, "Her home has an outer jungle, and inner jungle, and an inner inner jungle in which stalks at present the feline Marlene D. Lilly has prom-ised to introduce us, but so far no dice."

As I sat across from Ms. Messinger in her jungle shadowed office she appraised me with the sharp, practiced gaze of a medieval money changer and said with unassailable authority that my eyes were placed too high in my face (I shuddered), but that I had class, a rare quality those days (I relaxed slightly), and that she would take me on as an unofficial client (I silently cheered).

Lilly sent me out on quite a few job interviews, but I was defeated by my fear, extreme self-consciousness, and intense inhibition. My cold readings were just that—cold and read. I kept plugging away, but I was beginning to find my inexplicably frightened self a bit embarrassing.

I had no idea at the time why I was so withdrawn and scared at these auditions, which became a series of cool rejections. I'd walk in to meet the casting guys well prepared for the reading, but by the time I'd said hello, sat down, and picked up the script I'd freeze solid. I'd feel sort of mummified, bound up in invisible wrappings, severely restricted by forces I couldn't locate and fight. I was continually, exasperatingly, hopelessly defeated by an enemy I couldn't find.

I can see now that one of the most powerful factors in my emotional block in these situations was my unresolved relationship with my father. Though I was no longer living at home, I was still destructively attached to this man (or rather to my inner stories about him). My hatred and fear of Dad were virulent, even though I rarely saw him.

I projected these feelings onto every producer and director and casting agent I met. I unfairly turned these unsuspecting guys into my father, subconsciously fearing condescending judgments and suppressive sneers, certain that I could never measure up to their expectations. In reality the men behind these projected masks were merely hoping that I would fit the bill for the character in the show they were casting. Meanwhile my now permanently sober dad was happily bowling on the green in sunny Laguna Beach, completely unaware of the role I was writing for him in my self-generated struggles.

This is a near perfect example of how we endlessly torture ourselves and distort our lives with our own faulty thinking. There I was, a reasonably talented young actor trying to get work in Hollywood, ruthlessly sabotaging my efforts with distant memories of mean old Dad. My father was far away busily saving people in AA, but I couldn't help dragging him back into my life. In his absence I took on his role of suppressing and making me feel impotent. Dad was gone, but I couldn't let go of all my painful stories about the damage he'd done me and about my inadequacy in his presence. I continued to hate *him* even though *I* had assumed his nefarious ways.

We bamboozle ourselves with largely fictional stories all the time: My father despises me (how can I know that for sure?); anyone who really knows me couldn't possibly love me; my children don't appreciate me; my husband doesn't listen to me; my religion makes me better than you; they should have dealt with me fairly; I'm more important than you because I'm famous; I'm too addictive or stressed to quit smoking; life is so unfair; they should have taken better care of me.

Byron Katie, a savvy teacher I know, suggests putting our mental stories and beliefs to the test with three questions: (1) Can I really know this is true? (2) What do I get from this story or belief, what does it do for or against me? (3) Who would I be in the situation *without* this belief?

Then she suggests that we turn it all around and take full responsibility for all the stuff we're blaming on others. For instance, the story "You don't love me enough!" becomes "I don't love myself enough, and I don't love *you* enough." My story "My father suppressed and weakened me" becomes the much more accurate "I suppress and weaken myself with my thinking, and I also suppress my father by probably misunderstanding and misrepresenting him."

In other words, being a grown-up means taking responsibility for my own life and my own integrity. My father's integrity or lack of it is none of my business. My business is to come to understand the stifling fictions of my thinking and learn to prefer and honor reality, truth, what is.

Early in 1959 the fickle finger of fate began to stir things up in my life. Through AA, my father was acquainted with Jack Bailey, the loquacious host of *Queen for a Day*. Dad arranged for me to meet Jack and his agent, Alan Bernard, for lunch at the famous Brown Derby restaurant.

Alan Bernard worked for MCA, which was then the most powerful talent agency in the world (before MCA took over Universal Studios and was forced by the feds in an antitrust suit to divest itself of its agency business). With only feigned interest, Bernard agreed to set up an audition for me at MCA with two agents, Monique James and Ina Bernstein, who specialized in launching young performers. I was instructed to present a dramatic scene for them in two weeks.

I began rehearsing a scene with a rather strange young actress I'd worked with in Jeff's class, Adele. It was from an exotic fiction called *Rema of the Jungle,* and Adele played a beautiful wood sprite that I encountered and chased around an enchanted rain forest.

On the appointed day Adele and I arrived at the lavish MCA offices in Beverly Hills and were guided to a basement room filled, like the rest of the handsome pseudo-Greek building, with priceless antiques. Moments later Ms. James and Ms. Bernstein entered, chatted briefly, and asked to see our scene.

Adele and I rearranged gorgeous chairs and ancient tables to represent jungle trees and pools, and we romped somewhat edgily through our tropical romance. Sensing our nervousness, Ms. James asked us to play the scene a second time, which we did with a bit more verve. The two great ladies said very nice and we were dismissed.

I drove Adele home in exhausted silence, returned to my freeway abode, and spent the night in an agony of suspense.

Two endless days later Alan Bernard phoned me and announced with a tone of disbelief that Monique James, a major player at the agency, had recommended that MCA sign me on as a client! You could have knocked me over with a wisp of thistledown.

Because Monique was so respected (and feared) in the industry, the producers and directors she sent me to audition for greeted me with an interest and warmth I hadn't experienced before. This new friendliness gave me confidence, and I was actually hired to be an actor!

My very first professional job was one day's work on the long-running television series *Gunsmoke,* playing the part of a young punk cowboy who caused a lot of trouble in Dodge City. I'd never worked in film before and didn't know about the special techniques required in film: shooting scenes out of sequence (attending your victim's funeral before killing him), shooting scenes over and over again from different angles and distances, having to repeat all your movements exactly for each repeat, and hitting precise marks on every move. But I was so hyped up by the thrill of actually working on a film set with famous performers like James Arness that I caught on fast, and I don't remember making a single mistake. This miraculous feat of concentration used up at least a week's worth of energy, and I could hardly get out of my sagging pull-down bed for a few days afterward.

Susie Lloyd was a fellow student of Jeff Corey. We'd done several scenes in class together and had become good friends. Susie's father, Norman Lloyd, was a producer of television's *Alfred Hitchcock Presents,* and Susie invited me home for dinner one night with the hope that her father might cast me in one of his episodes.

The next week I was called to audition for an intense part playing one of Raymond Massey's sons in a Hitchcock television thriller. Getting that part was more fateful than I could have known. Ray Massey and I got on very well during the six-day shoot and the next year, based on this experience, he approved me for the biggest break of my life.

During the following months Monique found me enough interesting work in television to pay my modest bills. Of course I continued studying with Corey and Carolyn Trojanowski, my singing teacher.

Carolyn had become in many ways my mentor. She was a short, plump, dynamic woman with a lot of street smarts and considerable wisdom. She said I was too thin and should start working out with weights. I did. She said I didn't move very well and should study the rigors of ballet. I did. She said I could increase my energy by eating huge quantities of rare beef. For better or worse, I did.

Carolyn gave me psychological advice, too. Singing, next to lovemaking, is probably the most revealing human activity of all. You can fool people with speech and body language and charm, but the primal act of producing the sounds of song from deep within your body and heart (or not) will showcase your every fear, inhibition, reluctance, sensuality, joy, freedom, and love.

Though I had a good voice and could make pleasant sounds, my chronic and deeply buried fears and inhibitions severely limited the energy and the physical and emotional freedom that make singing worth listening to. You can't turn people on when you're turned off. The same problems of self-rejection and hiding behind a defensively "perfect" image that limited me in acting class were even more obvious to Carolyn as she observed my pleasant, but mightily inhibited, attempts at singing. Inhibition is the enemy of song. She guessed it would take more than musical technique to loosen me up psychologically.

Carolyn pointed out that I was promising but severely damaged goods and suggested that I see a psychologist she consulted from time to time named Linda Harris. My reaction was mixed. I didn't at all want my "perfect person" image to be penetrated. But I couldn't help being aware of my often intense discomfort and inexplicable inner pain. And lurking beneath all my denial and resistance was an immense curiosity not only about life but also about my own hang-ups. Working with Linda helped me to see that I wanted to know, to see truthfully, more than I wanted to hide and defend my shaky status quo.

My first session with Linda was in retrospect hilarious.

Linda: So, how is your life going at present?

Richard: Oh, great. I'm working occasionally and all sorts of good things are happening. I'm getting along just fine.

L: And your family? How's your relationship with your mother and father?

R: Mom and Dad are swell people. Dad's a popular speaker in AA, and Mom is gracious and lovely. We're just fine.

L: And you have close friends?

R: Oh, yeah, lots.

L: Your love life? How's that going?

R: Umm . . . Nice, exciting, sweet. Just fine.

L: I see. Tell me, Richard, why is such a perfect person like you, living a life that's "just fine," consulting a psychologist?

The implications of this question knocked the wind out of me. I'd been totally busted, and I had no idea how to reply. I couldn't understand why my charm wasn't working, why my act wasn't winning her over. It was as if this complete stranger, this attractive (she resembled the sophisticated and funny actress Mary Astor), cultured woman (the type I usually had great success with), far from being entranced, was calling me a liar.

I sat there stunned and dumb for some time, thoroughly shaken. Finally I admitted with great difficulty that despite my recent good fortune and my cheery exterior, I was disturbingly unhappy and conflicted, partly because my sexual orientation made me radically different from about ninety-five percent of the rest of humanity, and partly for shadowy reasons beyond my understanding. With this modicum of truth our good work began.

Fate's finger continued to stir. I was called to MGM Studios for a general interview by a young executive there whom I'd known slightly in high school. That meeting led to my playing the lead in a pilot film for a western television series called *The Paradise Kid* for NBC. Unfortunately westerns were on the way out at that time and the series didn't sell.

Years ago, long before television, MGM had produced twelve highly successful movies about the adventures of Young Dr. Kildare, starring Lew Ayres as Kildare and Lionel Barrymore as his mentor Dr. Gillespie. Unbeknownst to me, at the time of our *Paradise Kid* failure, the studio was developing a television series based on those old movies.

The producers had been searching unsuccessfully for months for a young actor, preferably unknown, to play the role of Kildare. In desperation they pulled the *Paradise Kid* pilot out of the vault and took a look. *Voilà!* For reasons unknown to me (the fickle finger having its way), they decided I was their guy. Apparently I had the qualities they were looking for.

My "big splash" was sailing into view, but there was one more sandbar to negotiate. The redoubtable Raymond Massey had already been cast as Dr. Gillespie, and because of his eminence he'd been given the power to approve the actor cast as Kildare. Thanks to the heavens and to Susie and Norman Lloyd, Ray had favorable memories of our work together in the Hitchcock show and gave his okay. With a mix of jubilance and panic I realized I had won the part—I shuddered and rejoiced. If I, an actor as green as grass, could manage to pull it off (a very big if), the *Dr. Kildare* television series would be my entrée into a brand-new life, the life of my wildest dreams.

STATUS AND PRESTIGE

I loved the challenges and joys of acting, but I was starving for the glitter of worldly "status" to fill my inner void. To paraphrase Mr. Henry: Give me applause or give me death!

In our culture, status—our state or condition in the eyes of *others*, our relative rank in the hierarchy of prestige—is perhaps the most fundamental preoccupation. I bought into our society's values and foolishly linked my well-being to the status conferred by "success" and celebrity. If I could get enough applause from enough people, my fears would disappear and I'd suddenly be just fine inside, happy as a lark, free as a bee.

In hitching my happiness to the slippery star of status like so many of us do, I failed to see the madness in my method. My well-being was completely dependent on the good opinion of *others* who could give it or take it away at will. I was giving my power, literally my *self*, away to the crowd.

I indulged in the popular illusion that one human being can have greater intrinsic value than another. The truth is that each of us is a unique, necessary, and incomparable aspect of spirit. Each life is a sacred part of the creative design and dynamic structure of life, of God. Given that truth (the ultimate wholeness of life), the illusion of "relative rank in the hierarchy of prestige" is totally irrelevant; it simply doesn't exist.

Human beings (and rocks and trees for that matter) are not just touched by divinity; we don't merely contain a divine spark within our otherwise sinful selves. Each of us *is* the divine, experiencing and learning and doing whatever we're doing each moment. It seems to me foolish to imagine that one aspect of the divine is intrinsically better or worse, higher or lower, than another. The drugged-out prostitute, the movie star, the potentate, and the archangel are all God itself exploring, creating, being, and learning. There is nothing but "God."

This premise in no way negates appreciating and striving for excellence, goodness, and compassion. Nor does it nullify aversion to brutality, harmfulness, greed, and such. It does not contradict our need for law and order, or even our appreciation of elites in all disciplines. It simply means that the hidden mud bricks that anonymously support the glorious gilt dome are, in the grand scheme of things, no less important or prestigious than the dome itself. It means that before I feel superior to the grubby homeless person I'm walking by, I'd better remind myself that I have no way of knowing why God has become and is experiencing life as that down-and-out being. I may just walk by, or I may offer money, or I may attempt to find shelter for this homeless guy. But even though I'm obviously better off than he is, the divine as me is no better than the divine as him.

The "humble nobody" knows this and has called his wayward spirit home. He may have striven for, won, and become attached to "somebodyhood," but has found its satisfactions short-lived and subtly hostile to those around him. He is free. Free to act rightly, to create lavishly, to love unconditionally, to do good unself-consciously, to embrace abundance with no need for labels or medals or even a whiff of prestige.

Back in 1960 on the verge of the *Kildare* phenomenon I was fiendishly hungry for any particle of prestige I could lay my hands on. I loved the work, but fame was my muse.

When we began filming the *Dr. Kildare* pilot on stage 11 at MGM Studios, a giant sprawl of real estate and dream-making facilities in Culver City, California, I was approaching the usually ripe age of twenty-five. But I was one of the slowest developers of all time, and I looked, felt, and acted a lot younger. In my still photos from the early years of the series I could almost have been a teenager.

Television networks like NBC and movie studios like MGM create and finance pilot films to sell projected series to advertisers. Everything depends on the success of the pilot. The networks schedule only potential winners.

I was of course aware of what was riding on the quality of our *Kildare* pilot, but I didn't dare give what was at stake (everything) a lot of thought. This was to be my portal to the glittering land of Somebodyness. I needed success, a spectacular success if possible, like a junkie needs a fix. At last my life would have value, and I might even be (dare I say it) loved.

Boris Sagal (a great guy and first-rate director) directed the pilot script, which introduced the characters of Kildare and Gillespie and their sometimes warm, sometimes adversarial relationship. Beverly Garland, a dramatic actress at the height of her considerable powers, was our first guest star. Our crew—camera, lighting, sound, wardrobe, set design, makeup—was an assemblage of superb technicians—terrific people. The project was smelling good. The only possible weak link was the inexperienced lead actor—*me*.

The usual shooting schedule of six days for an hour show was stretched to eight days for the all-important pilot. This was lucky for me because I hadn't yet learned to be Johnny-on-the-spot with my emotions, and I often needed a lot of takes to work up the requisite intensity, especially in the highly dramatic scenes. Extra takes eat up shooting time, and by the fifth day Boris Sagal lost patience and barked with considerable bite, "Okay, Richard, the honeymoon is over! Let's get with it!"

Chastened, I *did* get with it and stayed with it for the next five years. Boris's abrupt and derisive command in front of our whole crew and my fellow actors jolted me awake. Yes, I was genuinely inexperienced as an actor, but also I had been half-consciously indulging in a lot of neurotic baggage. My unacknowledged rage at life in general (for not being at all what I wanted it to be in my early years) had from the beginning taken the form not of explosive anger, but of the passive-aggressive stance of *I won't*. I'd pretend to agree, but inwardly I would not cooperate. This almost total resistance to life gave me an illusory sense of control. It also kept me in a kind of living death.

Boris's frustration shook me up enough to realize that I was sabotaging myself (and my desperate need for success) while fruitlessly "punishing" Boris, the father figure. In desperation I loosened the clamp I had long maintained on my emotions, and I called at least a temporary armistice in my war against authority. In other words, I started to get out of my own way and to become a professional.

Dr. Kildare was a rollicking success right from the beginning. The show was wildly popular all over the world and so was I (being identified by our vast audience with the sterling young doctor).

My hunger for recognition, attention, admiration, excitement, and adoration was satisfied a thousand times over. Fan mail poured in from everywhere, breaking studio records—twelve thousand letters a week. At birthdays and Christmas I was inundated with often charming gifts from fans as far away as Poland and Japan. The flash photos at public events were endlessly blinding. These were riches way *beyond* my wildest dreams. Even my relatively modest salary (I worked under a seven-year contract with MGM, the terms of which were set before the series' great success) seemed fabulous to me.

Such sudden and prolonged adulation can create monsters of the young and unwary. I was able to hang on to some sense of proportion partly because the work was so relentless (we shot thirty-six episodes the first year; today television series shoot about twenty-two), and partly because my still potent and unresolved insecurities kept me from foolishly believing that my public persona was the real me, that I fully deserved all the frenzied attention coming my way.

We worked twelve-hour days, and I still studied singing and dance several nights a week. Between seasons the studio would cast me in movies (*A Thunder of Drums, Twilight of Honor, Joy in the Morning*—none made it to the National Archives), and if any spare time remained, I was sent out on publicity tours all over the country. Weekends were spent learning the next week's script.

Fortunately I found the work exhilarating, and I loved the novelty of everyone thinking I was a somebody even if I couldn't quite believe it myself. My doubts remained even when I got to hobnob with genuine blue bloods.

A BRUSH WITH ROYALTY

It's interesting to observe how thoroughly addicted we are to creating and believing in hierarchies. We're endlessly calculating who gets to lord it over whom. I often ruthlessly judge my status relative to people I meet or even just observe from a distance, deciding who is better or worse. I do this so habitually that I barely notice the process, though I can acutely feel the results, which are distancing and closed-hearted and ignore the nonhierarchical nature of spirit.

Believing in hierarchical distinctions between the personal value of human beings can move us out of reality and into illusion. If we're not careful, we allow the constant hyping of celebrities, tycoons, political bigwigs, and even religious "authorities" to make us feel somehow inferior to all those "important" folks. I can't count the times that I have diminished myself in the presence of people I greatly admire.

In college I discovered the wonderfully witty plays and songs of Noel Coward and I was often asked to perform his musical whimsies at various student get-togethers. After *Kildare* ended, I even played Elyot in a tour of Coward's sublime comedy *Private Lives*. I was a devoted fan.

While I was living and working in London I took Sally Ann Howes to a big show-biz party where we were seated with Sean Connery and his wife at dinner. I thought that was pretty good, but then I looked across the room and saw Noel Coward talking with some friends and I nearly fell off my chair. When I could speak, I exclaimed to Sally, "My

God, there's Noel Coward!" Sally blithely replied that he was an old friend of hers and would I like to meet him?

Sally led me across the dance floor toward the great man—I followed fearing the worst. An actress I'd worked with in *Private Lives* had told me of meeting Coward at a party. The hostess had introduced her, "And this is Mary Robin Red." Sir Noel had glanced at her and said waspishly, "Of course you are," and turned away. I could imagine him saying all sorts of prickly things about young Dr. Kildare. But in fact he shook my shaking hand graciously and said, "Ah, Mr. Chamberlain, I've admired your work so much." Well, whether he meant it or not, I was struck dumb. I felt it would be ridiculous to lamely reply that I admired *his* work, too, so I just stood there like a blushing idiot. Luckily I was able to redeem myself at a later meeting. The point is that Coward was quite open to conversation while I strangled myself with my illusory mental story of his unapproachable greatness. I was oblivious to the fact that in a hierarchical sense he was just another human being.

One of the world's greatest fabricators of intimidating hierarchical illusions is England's Royal House of Windsor—the grand palaces and stupendously theatrical rituals are a form of hype so brilliant as to be thoroughly irresistible.

British royals were once the pinnacles of absolute political power in their expansive country, to be feared and obeyed. Today the royal family of Windsor has no political power at all; their duties are merely symbolic and ceremonial. It's true that during the horror of the Nazi blitzkrieg of World War II, the royal family stayed on in London through the incessant bombing and were hugely helpful in keeping the beleaguered English morale high. Yet they cannot be said to have been any braver than the millions of other Brits who lived and fought throughout the blitz. Still, despite recent scandal, the Windsors retain a tremendous mystique and are the very foundation of the ancient British class system. Without their king or queen, being a duke or earl or baron would have little meaning. Without their monarch, the Brits would *all*, heaven forfend!, be commoners. Most of us love the romance of pomp and circumstance and would feel diminished without the glittering the-atrics, proving the effectiveness of the royal hype machine.

In the early sixties, the immense success of *Dr. Kildare* gave me a taste of celebrity (the American version of royalty), which accorded me entrée into some royal high jinks.

Britain's Princess Margaret, young, beautiful, vivacious, and some-what reckless, was the Diana of her time. Around 1964, she and her hus-band, Lord Snowdon, arrived in the United States for a splendid tour involving Washington fetes, charity events, and a bit of frolic. The royal couple ended their tour in a Hollywood social whirl designed and exe-cuted by the princess's longtime friend Sharman Douglas. Sharman and Princess Margaret had met as girls when Sharman's father had been the U.S. ambassador to the Court of St. James.

The Hollywood crowd was ablaze, excitedly anticipating the advent of genuine royalty. Even I, busily at work on *Kildare,* was eagerly hoping for a chance to glimpse the fairy-tale princess and her consort.

Unbeknownst to me, my public relations agent, Rupert Allen, was deeply involved in the social arrangements for the royals and, through Rupert, Sharman Douglas asked that I be her escort to a huge charity ball honoring the princess. I was of course flabbergasted, but I decided to play it cool. I had heard that there was to be an "intimate" dinner party for Their Royal Highnesses at the Bistro restaurant, attended by only the triple-A list of show-biz luminaries. I told Rupert that I'd be delighted to escort Ms. Douglas to the charity ball *if* I could be invited to the Bistro bash. It worked! I was Sharman's escort to both events.

The Bistro party was, socially (and hierarchically), the high point of my life. The elite Hollywood crowd, including Elizabeth Taylor, Richard Burton, Rosalind Russell, Fred Astaire, Judy Garland, Frank Sinatra with Mia Farrow, Gregory Peck, Loretta Young, and others, had to be completely assembled before Princess Margaret and Lord Snowdon arrived. Everyone had what seemed like intense first-night jitters, and we all headed for the bar for a shot of liquid courage. Roz Russell, whom I'd never met before, nervously asked me if I thought her black dress was appropriate. Sinatra, beaming devastating charm, was the only seemingly unflappable star present. Maybe he was madly in love with Mia at the time and sailing on that blissful energy. Anyway, he buzzed with the same exuberantly devil-may-care vitality he had on-screen in his musicals. He wasn't afraid of anybody. The only person I've ever met whose charm had the impact of Sinatra's was Laurence Olivier. Olivier could broadside you with his charm the way a howitzer levels a Sherman tank. He had an inexplicable animal power that he could summon up at will. Once I was following him in a reception line meeting the cast backstage after seeing a play in London. Olivier bowled over each actor as we went along, making them, one by one, weak in the knees with his seemingly loving attentions. At one point he turned to me with a wink and whispered, "How am I doing?" He knew *exactly* how he was doing.

Finally the royal couple arrived, Princess Margaret gorgeous in a simple white dress and almost no jewelry at all. At the door she chatted briefly with Elizabeth Taylor, who was practically staggering under the weight of a spectacular tiara and pounds of diamonds and emeralds. Seeing them together was a comic lesson in contrast—dignity conversing with excess.

The party was a smash hit right from the start for everyone but Richard Burton. It seems there are gradations of status even among the triple-A glitterati. At dinner Elizabeth Taylor was seated by Princess Margaret at the front of the dining room, and Richard Burton was seated with me and four others at a table near the middle. Burton, a few sheets to the wind, complained bitterly to us about the indignity of his being forced to share our table so distant from the folks who really mattered!

After dinner everyone glided into another room with an orchestra and a dance floor. Princess Margaret was seated at a long table, and each guest was escorted to a chair opposite to her for a brief chat. When it was my turn to meet the princess, Laurence Harvey, very drunk, had squeezed in beside her a bit too close for comfort, so in order to escape she asked me to dance. I was thrilled to oblige, and we danced and chatted for a delightfully long whirl around the floor. I was enchanted by this lovely princess.

Later in the evening at the princess's request, Judy Garland sang and Fred Astaire danced and the magical merriment flowed late into the night.

Then the plot began to thicken. The next week during a session with Linda, my shrink, she related a very odd conversation she'd had two days before with a woman she'd sat next to on a plane from San Francisco. Somehow my name came up and the woman, whom Linda had not met before, said what a shame it was that a fresh young fellow like Richard was going to be invited by Princess Margaret to the Ranch. (If this were a movie there would be a doomy musical sting here.)

Rumor had it that at the end of their U.S. tour the royals would go with some friends to Sharman Douglas's father's ranch in Arizona for a bit of fun and frolic. The less friendly rumors hinted that the Ranch might be the scene of considerable overindulgences. Linda suggested that for the sake of my pristine reputation I'd be wise to sidestep such an invite if it indeed materialized. Nevertheless I was mightily intrigued.

Then came the big charity gala. I met Sharman and the princess at their hotel and was driven with them to the gala, where I was seated at a dinner table next to the still-powerful and regal gossip columnist Hedda Hopper. I'd first met Hedda during the early days of *Kildare*'s hot success. An MGM publicist took me to her Beverly Hills home for our first interview. We were shown into a cozy library, where a few minutes later the famous Hedda made a grand entrance and directed our attention to framed and signed photos on her walls, showing her being chummy with all sorts of movie luminaries. She was especially proud of a picture with the great swashbuckler Douglas Fairbanks, wearing his trademark tights. "Of course he padded," confided Hedda. "So did Barrymore as Hamlet. Of course most ballet dancers pad. With athletes it all goes to other places."

During our conversation at the gala I was stunned when Hedda said she'd heard I was to be invited by the royals to the Ranch. I gulped and replied that I'd heard the same. Hedda, whom I'd liked from the start, gave me a long, intense look and said, "You're getting into very deep water. . . . Can you swim?" This was obviously a veiled but strong warning, and though it greatly increased the aura of intrigue, I took it seriously.

The last royal party was a small dinner at the home of Rupert Allen. Again it was a stellar gathering, and again each of us was briefly seated by Princess Margaret for a few minutes of conversation. When my turn came, there was no mention of the Ranch. I was disappointed and relieved. Later I apologized for having to leave a bit early, but I had to be up at the crack of dawn for work. This would be my last visit with HRH and still no talk of the Ranch. As I went downstairs to the front door, Sharman suddenly came after me and in the privacy of the stairwell actually said the forbidden words, inviting me to the infamous Ranch.

What to do? I had longed for this mysterious invitation and was youthfully titillated by the rumors of sensual delights. But at the same time I sensed that this *was* very deep water I'd be jumping into, and I wasn't at all sure I *could* swim. For better or worse, caution prevailed and I regretfully declined, claiming the obligations of my work, thus leaving the mystery forever unsolved.

Sometime later while I was living in London during the late sixties and early seventies, I met Princess Margaret again several times at various theatrical events and receptions. I even met the queen at a reception following the premiere of *The Madwoman of Chaillot*. The queen asked me what I was doing in England. I said I'd just completed a six-hour version of Henry James's *The Portrait of a Lady* for the BBC. She said, "Oh, yes, we watched that."

"Wow, that's wonderful," I gushed.

"Well, not *all* of it," she replied, somewhat dampening my excitement.

I returned to London in the mid-1970s to play Prince Charming in *The Slipper and the Rose,* a musical Cinderella film directed by Bryan Forbes. Bryan and his lovely wife, Nanette, were friendly with the royal family, and he invited Princess Margaret and the Queen Mother to visit our set to watch the filming and then join us for lunch. I was given the huge honor of sitting next to the Queen Mother at lunch and found her legendary charm to be at least a match for that of Sinatra and Olivier. She was vivacious and interesting and even a bit sexy in her seventies. We actors were all in costume at lunch—I was wearing knee britches and long stockings. Bryan told me after lunch that the Queen Mother had said she thought I had great legs. That remains my favorite compliment ever—a touch of sauciness from perhaps the world's most delightful lady.

One evening during filming, Bryan and Nanette even arranged a "double date" with Princess Margaret and me. We picked up the princess at St. James's Palace. She and Lord Snowdon were separating at the time, and we certainly didn't expect to see him. But as we were about to leave the palace for a nearby restaurant, Snowdon (who was also friendly with the Forbeses and had been an unofficial photographer on *The Madwoman of Chaillot,* which Bryan directed) suddenly appeared. It was then I fully realized I was "dating" another man's wife. Snowdon was affably unpleasant, and we all felt rather awkward until we were able to leave. Though I felt a bit out of my league, the rest of the evening was enchanting. I waited for some mention of the mystery of the Ranch, but the princess uttered not a word.

I admit to being as dazzled as anyone else by the artful and artificial majesty of modern royalty. We're programmed by fairy tales and carefully contrived pageantry to place them on pedestals high above ourselves. Part of their mystique is that they embody our secret, childish dream of being loved and admired, not for our accomplishments and merits (most royals accomplish very little), but simply for what and who we are. The fantasy of being born into wealth unearned and position unmerited has allure, though the problems inherent in such careless largess are obvious (witness tales of wealthy woe in *Vanity Fair*). One way or another, the piper must be paid.

MY FAMILY REACTS

My family's reaction to all the sudden excitement of *Kildare* fame and my dancing with princesses was a complex mix, especially at first. My father had always been the unrivaled star and sovereign ruler of the Chamberlain Magic Show, a role enhanced by his achieving a kind of divinity in AA, where he'd become a sought-after speaker in AA circles even in Europe. He really *did* believe he was a "somebody" (a truly magical feat considering that he had, with sobriety, "transcended" his formerly troublesome ego). My mother was Queen Consort presiding over her lesser (in my father's opinion) domain of Al-Anon, and my older brother, Bill, was the handsome, vigorous heir apparent. I had always been the oddball; I never fit into the family hierarchy. I was around, but redundant. The eldest son was fulfilling most of his parents' dreams—if not scholastically, then in sports and socially with gorgeous girlfriends. He shone with good health and good looks and a penchant for reckless good fun. His shy little brother didn't hold a lot of promise.

My utterly unexpected blastoff into relatively stratospheric fame and fortune pretty much upset the chain of command. All at once my deluge of fan mail made Dad's yearly haul of Christmas cards seem paltry. Mom was demoted to being distant adviser to the new Prince Regent, and Bill, whom I'd always idolized (and whose friends had wondered how a twit like me could possibly be fabulous Bill's brother), was now becoming known as fabulous *Richard's* brother. The kingdom was in turmoil—vandals at the gates!

All this upheaval was a perfect laboratory where all of us could, if willing, examine the frantic workings of our respective egos. How illuminating it would have been for each of us to take a long look at our self-images, to see how we positioned ourselves in relation to one another and how attached we were to those positions. What an opportunity to see how much more importance we placed on the stuck solidity of our established pecking order than on the fluid, creative possibilities of love. Unfortunately I was too enthralled by the newness of my ascension and the family was too discomfited to do much introspection. Our souls remained, as far as I know, unsearched.

My parents' desire to protect their status quo surfaced in a prediction that my success, however undeniable, would be pretty much a flash in the pan and would shortly degrade for lack of substance. This rather unkind idea smoothed royal feathers, restoring some semblance of their former order.

When I'd visit my family, my father and I would get a B or maybe even a B-plus for good behavior, but a deep, unspoken abyss still yawned between us. Luckily on the *Kildare* set Raymond Massey and I were getting along like gangbusters.

Ray was a tall, big-boned, Lincolnesque gent with a big, resonant voice and an imposing presence, not unlike my father. He differed from Dad the farm boy in that he descended from a wealthy, influential Canadian family. Ray's brother had been governor general of our northern neighbor.

Ray's wife, Dorothy, was one of the first female corporate lawyers ever to break into that male bastion. She came from solid New England stock and was cultured, witty, and tough as nails. Both Ray and Dorothy played favorites—if they liked you, they were delightfully generous and loyal; if they didn't like you, run for cover! Fortunately they liked me, and I loved them.

Ray became a sort of surrogate father to me. Now that I think of it, our relationship mirrored the father-son kinship of Gillespie and Kildare. Even though I was such an inexperienced actor in the beginning, sometimes requiring more time and directorial attention than the rest of the cast, Ray never condescended to me and, as far as I can remember, never even showed impatience. Nor did he ever give me unrequested advice. He graciously treated me as if I were an old pro like himself.

The most severe test of Ray's fatherly indulgence came late in our first season. There was to be a lengthy scene in Dr. Gillespie's office in which Kildare was to deliver an endless monologue of obscure medical terms and complex information to Ray and a group of excellent character actors playing expert specialists who opposed Kildare's diagnosis. The speech was a minefield of technical medical jargon, almost impossible to learn, but I'd worked very hard on it. One of the medical terms was *epinephrine,* which I'd never heard of before and mistakenly pronounced e-PINE-e-frin.

We rehearsed the scene several times with me blithely pronouncing the fateful word e-PINE-e-frin, and all seemed to be going well. Then just before the first take, our script girl whispered in my ear, "Oh, by the way, darling, that word is pronounced epi-NE-fron," and I knew I was in big trouble

Partly because I was so pissed off that no one had corrected me earlier and given me a chance to practice this new pronunciation, I found it impossible to get through the speech. We shot it over and over again, and every time I came to *epinephrine* I froze up and blanked out. Even with cheater's notes written on my clipboard and everywhere else we could hide them, it took the entire morning to get the master shot. I was embarrassed beyond belief, but Ray never flinched, never looked disapproving or exasperated. The man was a saint.

Ray and Dorothy often invited me to their home for lunch or dinner when they were entertaining some of their notable friends, like actors Jack Hawkins, Christopher Plummer, and Sir Cedric Hardwicke. I'd sit like a kid and listen to the "grown-ups" telling marvelous tales of their theater and movie experiences. Once Sir Cedric looked at me keenly across the luncheon table and said, "You know, Richard, you've become a star before you've had a chance to learn to act." He meant this not as a dig, but as implied advice. It was partly because of this remark that I moved to England after *Kildare* ended, looking for solid acting training.

Every Saturday afternoon Ray and Dorothy lunched at their reserved table in the Polo Lounge of the Beverly Hills Hotel. Occasionally they'd invite me to join them. Along with their delightful conversation, the two invariables of these events were laughter and manhattans—lots of manhattans.

At one of these well-oiled affairs, Ray told me about an exclusive club he and Dorothy and several Old Hollywood luminaries like Tyrone Power formed in the glory days of moviemaking. The club was called IGMFU, which was the acronym for "I got mine, fuck you!" This was of course a grand joke, but not entirely. I've always suspected that IGMFU expresses the very essence of political conservatism. It is the creed of the far Right.

Also characteristic of Ray's humor was the inscription carved in their living room fireplace mantel. It was a play on the pretentious MGM logo, *Ars gratis artis,* which loosely translates to "Art for art's sake." Ray's version was *Ars gratis pecuniae,* "Art for money."

My friendship with the Masseys continued warmly, but intermittently after the *Kildare* show ended. In 1968, I flew off to England to acquire the acting training Sir Cedric had suggested I lacked. Unexpectedly I stayed abroad for four and a half years, happily working in television, the theater, and several feature films.

Some time after my return I was invited by Connie Wald to a luncheon for the Masseys at her home. As I arrived, Ray and Dorothy were slowly making their way from their car to Connie's front door—both using walkers! I suddenly and heartrendingly realized that age was having its cruel way with my treasured friends.

Perhaps a year later Dorothy died. I've never seen a man so utterly bereft and distraught as Ray. It was as if he'd lost the dearest part of himself.

Ray died not very long after Dorothy's passing. I spoke at his funeral about our wonderful friendship, about his being a second father to me. Afterward Ray's son Daniel (a splendid actor) told me how he envied my warm relationship with his father. As so often happens with fathers and their sons, Daniel and Ray had had stormy times.

Along with grief, I was grateful that life had given me a second chance to enjoy Ray's healing friendship. I had no idea at that time just how much more healing I would need, before I'd be able to "Get real!" as Jeff Corey had demanded.

Work on the *Kildare* series began to feel repetitive during the final two years. I was in a running dispute with our producers—I wanted Kildare to mature and embody more authority, while the powers that be were reluctant to mess with a winner. Occasionally when a really good script would appear, or when we'd have a great guest star, the old excitement would return. But generally I was feeling stuck and bored. I was longing for a chance to play new characters in films and the theater. I wanted to stretch and learn.

One of the highlights of our last year was the appearance of the queen of silent movies: Gloria Swanson. In her time Gloria Swanson was the most famous and the highest-paid actress in Hollywood and therefore in the world. When she traveled she'd reserve not a suite, but whole floors of the swankiest hotels. Decades later in her brilliant comeback film with William Holden, *Sunset Boulevard,* her spectacular performance seared her name once again in the gilded history books of cinema. She *was* big. *Sunset Boulevard* excepted, it was the *pictures* that got small.

For her appearance on *Kildare,* Swanson played a great and totally self-centered film star (what else?) who enters Blair General with a reparable medical problem and proceeds to drive the hospital staff nuts with her grand and demanding manner.

Even at her somewhat advanced age, Swanson's dynamic persona proclaimed in bright, flashing lights "movie star." She had a small, slim body and a great big exotic face with fierce, feline eyes and soaring brows. Her bright red mouth looked as if it might have indulged in a recent kill. Her trademark upturned nose should have been pixielike, but wasn't. She favored leopard-spotted prints.

Swanson was in great shape—she did a lot of yoga and loved to talk about all sorts of esoteric health enhancers. As fellow Aries, we liked each other right off and gabbed a lot between scenes. But I sure wouldn't have crossed her.

On her first morning's work with us she was to play a long scene in her hospital bed, with me doing bedside manner acting. After the second rehearsal she startled us all by yelling in her suddenly very large voice, "Hilda, *HILDA,* where is my breakfast?" Her real-life maid rushed on set with a large tray full of ornate breakfast things piled high with steaming goodies and coffee, which Swanson proceeded to down with relish as we all stood by and watched flabbergasted. This sort of delay was unheard of in the high-speed, cut-rate assembly line of television, but no one dared to peep. Just as in her heyday, Miss Swanson continued to breakfast on the set every morning.

In the course of our hospital story the character of Swanson's selfish actress becomes acquainted with a much younger female patient and the two become friends. When the actress, fully recovered, is about to leave the hospital she drops by her young friend's room to say good-bye and discovers the girl is dying. This was of course the climactic emotional scene in which Swanson realizes how much she cares for the girl, breaks down, and finally becomes a complete human being (such things happen in television).

Because this scene was so difficult and important for Swanson's character, we rehearsed it more than usual. On the final rehearsal Swanson indeed broke down and wept copious tears. We were all deeply moved, and I remember thinking with awe that if she could play the scene that fully in rehearsal she must have incredible reserves of emotion.

The makeup man repaired her makeup and the director said, "Okay, let's shoot it." Swanson, still recovering, jerked around saying, "What do you mean, 'Shoot it?' We just shot it!" Thinking the final rehearsal was a take, she had given her all. We filmed the scene several times, but, try as she would, her playing was never as full again, and she knew it.

I don't know when I've felt so bad for a person. I knew this performance, coming near the end of her legendary career, was probably one of this great actress's last. Only those of us lucky enough to be on set with her that morning would ever know how wonderfully well she'd played her final scene.

SELF-IMAGE

I've known actors and executives and just plain rich folks who, like Miss Swanson, expect everybody in every situation to know not only who they are but also how very important they are. And obviously I was indulging in some delusions of grandeur myself. Our mental images of ourselves can so easily slip into fiction, wishful thinking, or a safe, comfy rigidity. A contrived, inflexible, ego-serving self-image can stifle our relationships and diminish our aliveness.

Self-image is a mixture of who we *want* to be, who we think we *should* be, and avoidance of who we're afraid we *might* be. It is a product of our thinking, a complex of ideas strongly influenced by our culture's values and mores. Most of our self-images resemble a character in a play more than the spontaneous, moment-to-moment reality of our being. Self-image is a product of the past that can obstruct the direct experiencing of our lives right *now*.

I've observed that often when I meet a coworker, a friend, or even a loved one, it is a meeting of two self-images rather than an interaction of two open, unguarded, fully present beings. Habitually we subtly deceive each other, feigning interest, presenting attitudes and feelings that seem appropriate. I sometimes feel impelled to present myself as intelligent, kind, and caring when I'm feeling quite the opposite. And I'm so identified with my "improved" image that I don't feel at all dishonest. Nor do I usually see beyond the image being presented to me.

And our self-image overflows and makes demands on others. The executive expects to be obeyed, the guru expects to be worshiped, the beautiful expect to be pursued, the famous actor expects (needs) all sorts of recognition and favors and applause.

But what happens when the executive is challenged, when the guru is blasphemed, when the beauty is ignored, when the actor goes unrecognized? We feel hurt, angry, depressed, and vengeful.

After the enormous international success of *Kildare,* I was filming *The Madwoman of Chaillot* in Nice with a staggering cast: Katharine Hepburn, Danny Kaye, Charles Boyer, Yul Brynner, Giulietta Masina, Margaret Leighton, Donald Pleasence, Dame Edith Evans. During shooting we were all invited by Prince Rainier and Princess Grace to a splendid formal party at the casino in Monte Carlo. We arrived to the blazing flashes of the press and paparazzi clamoring for photos and interviews. Clamoring, that is, until I walked in. Not a single camera or mike pointed in my direction. This crowd of celebrity-crazed journalists looked past me as if I weren't even there.

Those of us who are consciously or unconsciously addicted to being famous gauge the heat of our precarious notoriety by how vigorously we're pursued by the press and paparazzi. I was shocked and bewildered—to be totally ignored by these dubious characters was to be deader than a doornail, quick-frozen, annihilated! All my years of clawing my way up the august ladder of "somebodyness," the whole carefully built structure of my newly worthwhile self (validated by international adoration), seemed at that moment to be flushed right down the toilet of crushed vanity. I was suddenly nobody. I made a beeline for the bar and got smashed. Doubly smashed, my ego was in tatters. (I was unaware of the fact that almost none of my work, including *Kildare,* had been shown in France at that time. The press had no way of knowing anything about me.)

An important question: What was smashed and who smashed it? The basic situation was this: We actors were simply a group of human beings walking into another group of human beings, all of whom were present to have a good time. From a spiritual point of view, if we were stripped of our contrived stories about ourselves, there was no hierarchical difference between any of us. We're all just beings living and learning and hopefully loving and creating and playing as best we can in a pretty tough world.

What thought process had formed in me the concept that I was a VIP who deserved (longed for) recognition, awe, and applause? Yes, I was a successful American actor whom my culture had deemed a "celebrity." Yes, I had been greeted with excitement at many events in the United States and Britain previous to this Monte Carlo party. Still, a wise person wouldn't have taken all this highly perishable adulation on as his *identity*. But I was too young to recognize the frailty and emptiness of a cultural value system that worships status. I ingested it whole hog. I needed to counterbalance the loneliness of my deeply ingrained self-dislike with grand illusions.

My true, image-free self was not smashed by being ignored by the French press—I was just a human being walking through a door. My precarious self-image had been hurt. The press didn't hurt me; *I* hurt me with an *idea* (my self-importance) based on two of my most cherished illusions: that public approbation would cure my ills, and that one person's divinity can exceed another person's divinity.

A fascinating example of self-image gone mad is the great film actress Joan Crawford.

JOAN CRAWFORD,
SELF-IMAGE
EXTRAORDINAIRE

When *Dr. Kildare* was at the height of its popularity, I was sent to New York during a brief break in production for a very fancy publicity event at the fabulous '21' Club. A lot of high-powered press attended along with several luminaries, the most luminous of whom was Joan Crawford. I'm not sure how they induced her to come, but there she was, radiant and slightly comic in a peculiarly Crawford getup: ankle-strap shoes and a purse made of the same fabric as her dress under clear plastic. Her dress was rather low cut for the afternoon and was designed to show off her still slim waist. To emphasize her monumentally sculptured face with its heroic, penciled brows she wore a big, sparkly necklace and topped it all off with a curiously shaped hat that might have come from the collection of Elizabeth II.

I was introduced to this great lady and asked her if she'd like something to drink—water, juice? She said, "A bullshot." A bullshot is a fairly mean concoction of vodka and beef bouillon. I ordered two, and we sat down for enough of a chat to discover that we liked each other.

Joan sort of "took me up" during the following days of PR interviews and appearances. We had an extravagant lunch (many more bullshots) at La Côte Basque where she spun out marvelous, sometimes ribald stories of Old Hollywood. Another day she invited me up to her incredible Fifth Avenue apartment (made infamous in *Mommie Dearest*) overlooking Central Park through the giant windows she'd had cut into the venerable building's façade.

Her teenage daughter Christina was there, behaving beautifully. Joan asked what I'd like to drink (water and juice weren't mentioned) and I said a gin and tonic, please. Joan turned to Christina and with stark severity ordered her to make two gin and tonics. Christina flashed a brief look of terror, almost curtsied and said, "Yes, Mommie," and expertly made our drinks. I had no prior knowledge of their relationship, but I couldn't help noticing that something frightening, even psychologically brutal, was going on between them.

Joan was immensely proud of her enormous apartment and showed me around with a kind of subdued glee. There was a lot of plastic. Some of her furniture and lampshades had plastic covers, and the fine wood of her dining room table was topped with a thick sheet of Lucite. Her dressing room was immense with several sets of ten-foot mirrored double doors that she flung open to reveal endless racks of dresses, coats, furs, ankle-strap shoes, and dozens of handbags, each specially made with the same fabric as a matching gown. Joan seemed to feel that her palace in the sky and these mountains of clothing were her crowning achievement, surpassing even her glittering career.

The next day Joan invited me to the Booth Theatre for a matinee of *A Shot in the Dark,* starring her friend Julie Harris and Walter Matthau. Joan had seen the play several times before but wanted to have yet another look at Julie Harris, whom she adored, perhaps to the point of a bit of a crush.

Joan's limousine picked me up at my hotel, and then we picked her up and arrived at the theater just before curtain time (Joan liked to walk down the aisle just as the lights were dimming so that everyone in the audience would see her but not have the chance to approach her).

Just before entering the theater, Joan stopped, turned toward her parked limo, and said, "Look," in a voice filled with reverence. I looked, but saw nothing to revere. Noticing my lack of awe, Joan said in a slightly exasperated, but still reverent tone, "The license plate." The personalized license said STEELE, the name of Joan's recently departed husband.

Sure enough, as we walked down the darkening aisle to our third-row seats all heads turned our way, people nudged each other, and there was an appreciative murmur.

During the performance Joan, whose metabolism apparently cranked on at a very high rate, kept busy cooling herself by dabbing cologne on her wrists and fanning herself with a clever little Japanese fan she'd brought in her dress-matching purse. At intermission Joan instructed me to follow her up the aisle a moment prior to the curtain hitting the stage floor so that she could get to the lobby and back herself against a wall before the audience had a chance to mob her. Feeling secure with her back protected, she graciously signed autographs for the clamoring matinee ladies.

This was my last outing with Joan—I never saw her again. Sure, she was a bit nuts, but I liked her a lot. She was spunky and tough, extremely talented, and, ultimately, touchingly sad.

It seemed to me that she had devoted (quite successfully) her entire life, her total focus, to securing the grand edifice of the arduously crafted *image* of Joan Crawford. Like me in earlier days, she had become so helplessly ensnared in the loony values and fantasies of fame that her soul languished from inattention.

Joan Crawford hit the exhilarating heights and stayed aloft for decades, but the inevitable skids took her by surprise and left her grounded, alone, and without alternatives. I wonder if Lucille LeSueur, the girl who became Joan Crawford, ever had a chance in life at all. Perhaps, ignored by her alter ego, she expired long before Joan Crawford finally faded away.

Is it possible to experience the deep satisfaction of creativity, the abundant rewards of success, without losing one's inner nobody? To achieve renown in one's chosen field while remaining just a person among fellow persons? To cease comparison and even competition altogether? To discover one's strength and wisdom without labeling oneself *strong* and *wise*? Is it possible just to *be*? I suspect that among angels, those beings of pure love, there is no self-congratulation at all. They radiate love simply because that's what they are. Can we do that, too? Even for a moment?

BEYOND *KILDARE*

After five glorious years, the *Dr. Kildare* series ended. Our cast of regulars and our marvelous crew had become a close family during our years together, and our farewells were sad and tearful. I knew I'd remain friends with Raymond Massey who lived nearby, but crews scatter far and wide when a show ends and it was unlikely I'd see many of them ever again.

Kildare had been an incredible break for me, and a grand, if grueling, rocket ride. Though I was considered more a heartthrob than a serious actor, it had put me on the map, and I'll always be tremendously grateful for such a dazzling and educating experience. That said, it was time to move on—onward and *upward* I hoped.

For about a month after we shut down I was deliriously happy to be free of the grind, free to explore new opportunities. On the thirty-second day I woke up with a start, jolted by the fact that I was now just another out-of-work actor. I crashed and burned for a time. I found that my happiness, my whole sense of self, was totally attached to and dependent upon being successfully employed and in demand. A brief holiday was one thing, being jobless was quite another. An actor without a job has no assurance that he'll ever be employed again. I felt a dull panic not unlike imminent death. I put on a brave front and went about life with friends and art projects and movies and such, but I was getting scared.

There were offers for some new television series that perked up my spirits a bit, but I turned them down because I had big ideas about expanding into features and theater. I did several summer stock productions to get some theatrical training, but the brief rehearsal periods (usually about one week) didn't allow much exploration. Then I was offered *Breakfast at Tiffany's,* a big Broadway musical with Mary Tyler Moore as Holly Golightly. Abe Burrows was writing and directing, David Merrick producing, Bob Merrill was doing the music, and Michael Kidd was choreographing. It sounded too good to pass up so I leapt in.

After rehearsing in New York, we opened for a month's run in Philadelphia to mixed reviews. The gypsies and probably just about everybody else in the production started to smell trouble early on. I was oblivious and having a ball. When we played another month in Boston amid constant script and song changes, even I began to see dark problems looming.

Edward Albee (who made *that* choice?) was brought in to rewrite the show, and while he charmed us all personally, he transformed our lighthearted musical into a dark and rather gloomy semiopera.

After Boston we closed for two weeks to rehearse Albee's new material and finally opened to previews on Broadway. Well, with the exception of parts of *Oklahoma!,* New Yorkers had never seen a dark and gloomy musical before and they hated us. They shouted rude remarks and walked out in droves. Merrick closed *Tiffany's* after just four previews with a self-serving announcement in the *New York Times* saying he was losing a bundle but wanted to save New York from a lousy show. Despite a huge advance ticket sale, we closed before we opened.

I'd never known professional failure before and I was stunned and heartbroken. Mary gave an emotional closing night party at Sardi's. Around two in the morning, I staggered out on the street and walked drunkenly to our theater to see my name "up in lights" for the last time. I'd had such high hopes for the show—it was like losing a dear friend. I broke down sobbing. And to further complicate things, my self-image was in big trouble—I needed a major overhaul. I thought I was finally a big star, beyond failure. What was going on?

I limped back to Los Angeles, my frazzled tail between my legs, and sought the consultation of old friends. Show business veterans like Angela Lansbury, Gower Champion, and Ruth Gordon assured me that failure was an integral part of our business, and that it was good for me to experience a whopper of a flop early in my career. My wounds healed more quickly than I expected.

THE SEVENTIES

One of the exciting and scary things about an acting career is surprise—you never know what's going to happen (or not happen) next. Following the dreadful demise of *Tiffany's*, the hot, innovative young film director Richard Lester, who followed up his groundbreaking Beatles film *A Hard Day's Night* with a witty comedy called *The Knack* and the Beatles' second film, *Help!*, asked to see me in London about a part in his new film, *Petulia*. It was to star Julie Christie, George C. Scott, and Shirley Knight. I got on a plane posthaste. Meeting in his office, Lester said he wanted me for the part of Julie's neurotic, sometimes violent husband, David. He described the character as "a great-looking, but empty Coke bottle" and said with a wry half grin that he thought I'd be perfect. I felt the dig and instantly worried that my Magic Show might be slipping; but the man was offering me a swell job. With a wry half grin of my own, I said yes.

This would be my first serious film, my first job as a grown-up, my chance to graduate as an actor into the real thing.

We filmed *Petulia* in Sausalito (before that charming seaside town was choked by tourists) just across the Golden Gate Bridge from San Francisco. It was 1967 and the hippie scene was in full flower—so many beautiful, open-faced young people everywhere, gliding through their lives in a rainbow haze of almost angelic loveliness before the drugs took their toll. Here's part of a letter I wrote to Joe about living in Sausalito:

Life is fantastic here. My boathouse is tied up right at the tip end of the pier, with a splendid view of San Francisco Bay and various islands and peninsulas. It's a rather rustic affair built on a rectangular barge, consisting of a front sundeck, one good-sized room with a fireplace made from an old, rusty, round buoy with a laughing mouth cut in it. . . . I could sit here, bobbing as the boats go by, watching fingers of fog advance and retreat over the various hills, drinking home-brewed beer (a gift from my landlord) and stoking old Laughing Buoy forever.

Janis Joplin and the Grateful Dead in all their soulful, Southern Comfort–drenched glory were in the movie. We filmed their scenes during all-night marathons in the Fairmont Hotel lobby in San Francisco. When we finished at dawn we'd all drive back to Sausalito, have a blurry breakfast by the sea, and find our way back to our houseboats for an all-day sleep. The whole shoot was an utterly magical time *and* I got to play rough with Julie Christie!

Working with Julie was amazing. She was the most beautiful woman I'd ever laid eyes on. Though rather small, she somehow had the majestic, untamed quality of a wild horse. I found her to be the most gorgeous, fascinating, professional, unpredictable, charming, bright, bullying, feminine, haunted, funny, frightening creature I'd ever met.

We seemed to be working well together, though I didn't have the faintest idea how my work in the picture was going. Richard Lester was a marvelous director—though quite mysterious and complicated. He pushed his actors in very odd, unexpected directions, and you found yourself doing things you hadn't imagined at all. As puzzling as all this was at first, I think Lester helped me break through the somewhat calculated approach I had brought to my craft. At least in my art, if not in my life, I was allowing some spontaneity to break through my iron control.

Julie was living with her British boyfriend (almost as beautiful as Julie) on a very grand houseboat just down the bay from my much smaller one. I liked him, and they seemed a perfect couple. But Warren Beatty was in town and on the prowl. He circled around Julie for a time and then pounced. Warren, in his voracious prime, was irresistible; Julie succumbed.

Though I admired his intelligent tough-guy acting, I didn't get to know George C. Scott at all. Between scenes he would retire to his dressing room trailer to smoke cigars and play poker with his cronies. I suspect that beneath his sizzling bravura he was rather shy.

Richard Lester, who pretended to be a Brit himself, had found a way around Hollywood unions and assembled an almost totally British crew for *Petulia*. Being in the charming company of so many English folk solidified a plan I'd been considering for some time. I wanted to expand my horizons by getting some solid acting training, and the famous acting academies in London seemed the place to find the most inclusive curriculum. Shortly after making *Petulia* I rented my house in L.A. and took off for England.

Once again fate's finger began to stir. The day after I arrived in London my agent at William Morris said the BBC was looking for an American actor to play Ralph Touchett in a six-hour television production of Henry James's novel *The Portrait of a Lady*. I quickly read the book (as quickly as you can read a thousand pages of James's brilliantly complex writing) and loved both the story and the tragic character of Ralph. I signed on for what was to be a wonderfully intense learning experience. Working with James Cellan Jones, our superb director, and the excellent cast taught me more in a short time than I might have learned in formal training at one of England's famous acting schools. This on-the-job training continued the entire four and a half years I lived and worked in England.

Peter Dews was running the legendary Birmingham Repertory Company and directing many of its productions at the time. The company was running a small deficit, and Peter was looking for a well-known actor to play Hamlet—someone who might perk up their box-office sales. One night Peter and his wife, Ann, were watching *The Portrait of a*

Lady on the BBC and he turned to her and said, "There's our Hamlet!" Ann fell off the sofa laughing at this absurdity, but Peter persisted. To my total amazement he offered me one of the greatest and most elusive characters in dramatic literature.

I worked fervently on the play for weeks with several teachers; all of them advised me as diplomatically as possible to avoid embarrassment and decline. With enormous regret I asked my agent to turn it down.

The night before my negative decision would be final I awoke in a sweat saying out loud "I've got to do it! I've got to do it!" We called Peter the next day and said if he would agree to work with me on the part for a couple of months before we went into actual rehearsal I'd give Hamlet my best try. He said he would, and I took the terrifying leap.

Though Peter taught me a great deal about playing Shakespeare during those two months, the first five weeks of rehearsal were a desperate trial for all of us. The splendid actress Gemma Jones was playing Ophelia, and her performance grew more and more exciting by the day. I was working like a fiend, but my habitual fears and inhibitions kept me tied in knots. At the end of the fifth week Peter called me into his office in despair. "What are we going to do? I'm at my wit's end. It just isn't happening," he almost moaned. Shaken, I replied that I thought when we got into run-throughs the sixth and final week that I'd begin to pick up steam. Having no alternative, Peter agreed.

And, thank God, I did begin to come alive as Hamlet the final week of rehearsal. At last things were looking up, until the day before opening night, when quite by accident I found out that all the London critics would be coming up to Birmingham to review this upstart American interloper. I thought we were far enough away from London to be safe from media surveillance. This news that the critics were storming our gates struck me like The Hammer of Doom.

Before the opening night curtain, the general expectation of disaster was so tangible in our ancient theater (the Birmingham Rep until this moment had had a glorious history) that you could almost reach out and touch the tension. This malign atmosphere crept into my body, voice, and mind like a malevolent demon. I managed to get through the first scene croaking my lines in a strangled voice and strutting around stiffly on legs that couldn't seem to bend. But in the next scene when Hamlet is told of the appearance on the battlements of his great father's ghost, I dried up completely, and my terror left me deaf to all prompting. Finally after what seemed like hours of silence, my memory resurrected and I was off and running.

Instead of ridiculing my performance, which I was later told they had come to do, the critics seemed to find my eccentric interpretation (distorted as it was by terror) rather novel and interesting. Most of their reviews were quite good. Thanks largely to Peter Dews's patient tutoring and direction, I had actually pulled it off.

Having graduated from pretty boy to actor, I was at last taken seriously, and it was an exhilarating experience. Some fascinating work followed *The Portrait of a Lady* and *Hamlet.* Ken Russell cast me as Tchaikovsky in his bizarre film *The Music Lovers,* with the astonishing Glenda Jackson. I played Octavius Caesar in a dreadful film of Shakespeare's *Julius Caesar,* with Charlton Heston as Antony and Jason Robards (who saw straightaway that the film was a loser) as Brutus. Robert Bolt cast me as Lord Byron in his film *Lady Caroline Lamb,* which also starred my great friend Margaret Leighton. At around the same time, I traveled to Nice to work with Katharine Hepburn in *The Madwoman of Chaillot. Madwoman's* producers were the last of the big spenders, and we were all put up at the fabulous La Voile d'Or Hotel in Cap Ferrat, one of the most gorgeous places on earth. A good deal of this movie was shot outdoors, so they had to keep one indoor scene called a "cover set" ready in case of bad weather. The cover set was a long scene between me and Donald Pleasence, and since the weather stayed sunny we got to hang around the south of France for the entire three-month shoot—the ultimate working holiday!

One clear Sunday afternoon I climbed out of the chilly Mediterranean after a long swim and headed toward the hotel. It was still off-season and the veranda was empty except for three august figures sitting at a small table with a bottle of champagne. The three were Katharine Hepburn, Danny Kaye, and Federico Fellini.

Fellini was married to Giulietta Masina and had been visiting his wife and our production for several days.

Fellini was at the height of his fame as Europe's greatest film director, having taken the world by storm with a number of marvelous and innovative movies. These included the unforgettable and rather surreal *8½,* and *Juliet of the Spirits,* which was full of symbolism delving deeply into Juliet's unconscious mind. His frequent appearances on our film set wearing a very theatrical flowing overcoat and broad-brimmed hat were unnerving to say the least for our director, Bryan Forbes. It was rather like trying to play a round of golf with Tiger Woods looking over your shoulder.

As I approached, still dripping from my swim, the mighty three asked me to come sit with them and I happily did. This was a once-in-a-lifetime trio worth listening to.

Their conversation had become a bit heated. Hepburn, who as usual was doing her best to hide her real femininity in army fatigues, was saying, "Oh, Federico, your early movies were just fine, straightforward, realistic. But then, like that crazy Picasso, you've gone berserk. I mean, that absurd *Juliet of the Spirits*? What on earth was that all about?"

I was so shocked that anyone, even Hepburn, would dare speak like that to the high potentate of world cinema that I barely heard what followed. Anyway, Kate, having finished her pronouncement, stalked off to her villa. She liked to dine and be asleep by eight o'clock.

Watching Kate climb the stairs and disappear, Fellini said with a touch of sadness, "She is afraid of the night. She is afraid of her dreams."

I played Hamlet again in an entirely new production for Hallmark Television. Again this was a huge stretch for me, because Sir John Gielgud, one of the greatest Hamlets ever, played the Ghost; Sir Michael Redgrave was a very dotty Polonius; and the great Margaret Leighton played Gertrude. One day on the set Sir John asked me what other Shakespearean parts I'd played. I said sheepishly, "None," to which he replied imperiously, "*I* never played any of the smaller parts either." Also during my stay in England we filmed Norman Rosemont's television movie *The Man in the Iron Mask* in France. The rarest treat of that production was working with another of the British acting greats: Sir Ralph Richardson.

Though I returned to the States for work several times during my years in England, I was growing more and more attached to my British friends and to the ancient culture of that sceptered isle. America seemed young and brash by comparison, and I thought for a time that I might stay on permanently.

Two factors changed my mind. By the beginning of my fifth year as an apprentice Englishman, I was starting to feel like a welcome visitor at a club to which I would never fully belong. Then the clincher: During a meeting in London with a Hollywood director, he asked (noticing the slight British accent I'd acquired by osmosis) if I thought I could still play American parts. Flash!—It was time to go home.

Packing up my apartment overlooking Hyde Park was an extremely sad business. This wasn't just any move—I knew I was ending an incredibly rich and importantly creative era of my life and inevitably distancing myself from my much-loved London friends. It was a bit like dying.

And yet, once I was resettled in the little hillside house I bought in L.A. during my *Kildare* days, and reconnected with my L.A. friends, I was glad to be home.

Feature film and television work was plentiful if occasionally below snuff. I did two features for the hot producer of disaster movies, Irwin Allen. The big one was *The Towering Inferno,* starring Paul Newman *and* Steve McQueen, Faye Dunaway, William Holden, Fred Astaire, Jennifer Jones, Robert Wagner, and O.J. Simpson. Irwin Allen had two great gimmicks. He would hire as many name stars as he could lure with big bucks, and he would use first-class special effects.

Inferno was shot almost entirely on one huge ballroom set where the characters were all trapped by fire. It was amazing to watch all these huge stars hanging out together, shooting the breeze between scenes. As I remember, a fair amount of beer was downed during these gab sessions. Usually the big names hung out together, but I noticed that classy Fred Astaire seemed more comfortable talking with the crew.

Though I knew Paul Newman socially, I had never worked with him before. I was surprised by the intense arguments that sprang up between him and the director just before shooting each of his scenes. After a few days of this I guessed they had a sort of unspoken agreement to get fighting mad at each other before each take in order to get Paul juiced up for his scene. This acting technique was new to me.

My character was the villain responsible for the catastrophic fire. I made the big mistake of playing him like a jerk from the beginning instead of keeping his nefarious nature disguised in strong good-guy clothes until his evil deeds were finally exposed.

Steve McQueen's performance was a stunner. His part as written was just inches away from dreary. But with his flashing blue eyes and his rare superstar charisma as well as his enormous savvy as a screen actor, Steve transformed his standard fire chief character into a star vchicle. As disaster films go, *The Towering Inferno* was a winner.

My second film for Irwin Allen, *The Swarm,* was somewhat less towering. It was studded with stars of a slightly older variety: Henry Fonda, Richard Widmark, and José Ferrer. We were all fighting off hordes of killer bees invading the United States from South America.

Computerized special effects hadn't yet hit their stride so we used real bees. Thousands of these little critters were kept in refrigerated railway cars. The cold made them drowsy and slow, enabling a bunch of expert women chosen for their small hands to gently squeeze each bee belly and snip off its stinger. During our death scenes hundreds of these newly revived, but stingerless bees were poured over us as we writhed and screamed and at last expired in feigned terror and pain. Having those insects crawling over my face and down my neck into my clothes was a sensation not easily forgotten.

José Ferrer, a great actor who came to fame in his superb film portrayal of Cyrano de Bergerac, was (like most of us) a bit ashamed of being in this B bee movie no matter how much Irwin Allen was paying. One day as we were waiting to shoot a particularly embarrassing scene, he said in a mock theatrical voice, "Ah, Richard, I've whored in television, I've whored in movies, but I've never whored in the *theater!*"

To balance my film work I tried to do as many plays as possible. Word had gotten out about the Birmingham *Hamlet,* and the Seattle Repertory Company asked me to play Shakespeare's *Richard II,* a splendid role that I took on a second time in a quite different production at the Ahmanson Theatre in Los Angeles directed somewhat arbitrarily by Jonathan Miller. Jonathan detested King Richard and loved his nemesis Bolingbroke, so I had some interesting problems this second time around. Also at the Ahmanson I played Cyrano de Bergerac and Shannon in *The Night of the Iguana.*

Around this time Richard Lester, whom I'd loved working with in *Petulia,* asked me to play Aramis in his witty version of *The Three Musketeers,* with Michael York, Oliver Reed, Faye Dunaway, Raquel Welch, Charlton Heston, and Christopher Lee. I jumped at the chance to play debonair Aramis, the ultimate hypocrite who, while pretending to be deeply religious, was seducing every damsel in the parish.

Musketeers was shot in a variety of fascinating Spanish locations, like Seville and Toledo—an education in itself. And the high romance of the story coupled with the often hilarious swordplay and the colorful personalities of the cast made this a dream job.

Raquel Welch was a revelation. She didn't arrive on set until about three weeks into production and was preceded by a gale of unpleasant rumors. While the rest of us had formed a rather jolly group willing to rough it a bit, it was said that Raquel was demanding all sorts of perks like a dressing room painted a special color filled daily with flowers, and she insisted that she be addressed on the set by us all as "Miss Welch." It was generally agreed that we were going to hate her guts.

When "Miss Welch," having just flown into Madrid, was to deign to visit our set, we were not thrilled. Not, that is, until she arrived in a soft blue denim outfit showing lots of perfect skin and looking so gorgeous she took our combined breath away. She smiled dazzling smiles and said sweet, friendly things with a simple charm that absolutely captivated us all. In five minutes we were enslaved. She was in like Flynn.

Raquel gave one of her best performances as Michael York's accident-prone lover. She handled her almost slapstick part with good humor and finesse. She was gorgeous *and* funny.

Oliver Reed was the one to be wary of. While he could in his own way be as charming and friendly as Raquel, he was in fact a rough-and-ready barroom scraper, tough as nails, and dangerous.

Oliver had incredible stamina. His studio drivers hated driving for him because he'd be out all night every night boozing and roughing up people and eating live goldfish out of restaurant aquariums. Yet he was always on set on time every morning, his lines down pat, giving his usual first-rate performance. I haven't the foggiest idea how he did it.

In our endless sword fighting scenes Oliver was very rough with the Spanish stunt men, kicking them around something fierce. Of course, the stunt men had to be very careful of the actors and were forbidden to fight back except as choreographed. During a staged fight near the end of shooting, one of the stunt guys "accidentally" stabbed Oliver for real. His sword point entered Oliver's hand just below his wrist and came out halfway up his arm. It was a very nasty wound that put Oliver in the local hospital for several days. We all suspected it wasn't accidental at all—we sniffed revenge.

The screenplay for *Musketeers* was unusually long and divided into two halves by an intermission. I thought, well, if an intermission worked for *Cleopatra* with Taylor and Burton, why not for *Musketeers* with Welch and York? It wasn't until *Musketeers* was released as *two* movies, *The Three Musketeers* and *The Four Musketeers,* that we realized our producers, the Salkinds, had paid us all for one film and then turned around and sold it as two films. Luckily there was something in Raquel Welch's contract that allowed us to threaten legal action, and the producers agreed to pay us for the second film. Actors' (already voluminous) contracts now include an additional "Salkind" clause forbidding this scam.

In my experience all acting jobs are hard serious work, but *Musketeers* was great fun, too. Richard Lester was a fount of funny story ideas, the actors were all amusing people as well as first-rate performers, the locations were fabulous, and my horse never threw me. I returned home to Los Angeles happy and optimistic, a sure sign that challenges were in store.

DISCOVERING LOVE

In L.A. in the early seventies, everything was just fine on the outside—I had good friends and interesting work, and the fame and admiration I'd worked so hard and been so lucky to achieve. But inside, my old fears and deep insecurities remained curiously unabated. I was still living my life as a prelude to the *real thing* that I imagined would happen somewhere in the future, when some kind of magical kiss would turn this frog into a prince. In relationships I had to be always right and in control. If I lost the upper hand I was afraid that I'd be overwhelmed. I couldn't really commit to anyone—I kept one foot out the door, ready to escape when things didn't go my way. I could like, but I couldn't love.

My acting was still overcalculated—there were wonderful moments, but I sometimes didn't trust myself enough to consistently allow the kind of spontaneity that makes really exciting performances. It was a baffling disappointment that my prayers for success, having been generously answered, left me so unexpectedly incomplete. I seemed to have it all, yet I was vaguely aware of having very little of whatever it was (I wasn't sure) that was of real importance to the art of living.

One afternoon I was standing in my kitchen, on the phone, discussing these dissatisfactions with Johanna Ray, one of my dearest friends. Johanna suggested I see a Gestalt therapist she knew named Don Barenfeld. She hadn't gotten on with him, but she thought I would. I began working with Don both privately and in group therapy.

Group therapy was a revelation—especially for an actor observing

human nature. It offered an intimate view into what makes us tick, to
see how alike we all are. Watching people work through resistance,
denial, and ignorance into the truth of how they defeated themselves
with fictional stories and beliefs about themselves and others was a revelation. Seeing warmth and vitality flow back into their faces when they
stepped through their fear and owned up to the truth (the beautiful
truth) of what they would have called their own shit was deeply moving. Truth is the alchemy that turns our shit to gold.

However, it took me several months to dare to move from observer
to participant. During the early weeks of group, I experienced an odd
dichotomy in myself. I could fully see and appreciate the beauty of
Don's work with everyone else. I was excited to watch people drop their
negative stuff and begin to bloom. I had on some level a considerable
understanding and appreciation of this healing process, but I remained
too proud, too passive-aggressive, too frightened of fessing up to my
own shit to actively join in the process myself. I couldn't break out of
my habitual, fiercely guarded self-image of charming perfection. Again,
I was unable to commit to being a fallible human being. After weeks of
silence in these group sessions, Don aptly described me as dying of
thirst in a sea of Evian.

During our halting work together Don took two weeks off to attend
a workshop at Sky High Ranch in the Mojave Desert with a very interesting spiritual teacher named Brugh Joy. When he returned he was
remarkably changed. He seemed much softer, more present, and far less
abrasive. Don told me about Brugh's work, and I was so intrigued I
signed up for his next workshop, a seventeen-day retreat with about
thirty people. The desert ranch was spare and starkly beautiful, the people were varied and bright, and Brugh was (perhaps literally) a godsend.

A page full of superlatives couldn't exaggerate the importance of
this workshop to the unfolding of my life. Up to this time love and compassion were real to me only within the safe environment of acting. Dr.
Kildare's most luminous quality was his compassion for his patients,

and as an actor I could embody his caring nature (which was not entirely alien to my own nature, however deeply buried it was). But in my daily life my heart remained tightly shut within protective walls of fear. I distrusted myself and therefore couldn't begin to trust anyone else. Until you lovingly embrace your own existence, you have no context in which to love another person or the world or indeed life itself.

So there I was, driving up to the high desert, a clenched fist fiercely clutching the imagined safety of my habitual life, quite blind to the warm human caress of love. Though I couldn't have said or even been aware of this at the time, love was in fact unknown to me. And yet I urgently longed for exactly that. Fortune smiled. Brugh's genius was in facilitating the opening of our hearts to love.

Brugh Joy (the name is for real) had been a brilliant medical doctor who found in the course of his practice that he could feel the various qualities of his patients' energies with his hands at a slight distance from their bodies. He also found that he could channel healing energy through his hands to his patients. These gifts, combined with his spiritual insights, drew him away from traditional medicine into teaching and spiritual healing.

Sensing these subtle energies and channeling healing energy (essentially love) were a central part of our training at the workshop. Being highly competitive in pursuing personal status of any kind, and harboring the vanity of secret hopes for spiritual superstardom, I, of course, couldn't feel or do any of it. Others in the group progressed well right from the start, and my ineptitude was extremely painful and humiliating.

For the first few days I was embarrassed and angry with Brugh. I actually stalked out of one session, raging against the whole process, feeling (quite symbolically) sharp chest pains in the area of my heart. I was at war with myself. My habitual, controlling self-image fought for its survival against the urgings of my heart toward openness and freedom.

Brugh was also a master orchestrator of *group* energies. As we gradually got to know one another and became more immersed in our work and play together (surrounded by the subtle majesty of the desert landscape), we coalesced into a warm, unified group of inquiry and discovery. Our individual personalities, problems, and points of view, while remaining intact, melded into the various notes of a kind of humane music. Little by little our particular aspirations grew to include everyone (even the inevitable person whom you find intensely annoying).

A typical workshop day began before six o'clock when we all got up and in solitude watched the desert sunrise. Shortly after sunrise, we gathered in a large, pillow-lined living room for morning meditation followed by a delicious breakfast in a dining room that overlooked a vast panorama of the desert valley below and the purplish mountains beyond. After about an hour of free time, we would gather in the meeting room and lie down on the carpeted floor and listen to a piece of classical music played at high volume. Brugh believed the music elevated and energized the work session to follow. He then gave a talk and discussed our dreams, and we had a general conversation about our current work. The afternoons were usually free for desert exploration, individual "inner" work, or spiritual reading. Another group meeting followed dinner, after which we'd all return to our cabins for an often too brief night's sleep. Many of the group meetings involved "energy work," which taught us about the subtle energy fields that emanate from our bodies. We learned to sense, from another person's body as well as from our own, a concentrated flow of energy from various points on the body. Those who could do this learned to sense imbalances in others and learned to correct these imbalances with energy that flowed from their own hands, often without actually touching the body.

If this seems difficult to understand, think of people you know who give wonderful hugs or massage therapists who have that special "healing touch." Whether they know it or not, these people are also working with healing energy that naturally flows from them to you. For example, when you have a headache, a common gesture is to place your hand on your forehead for immediate soothing. The hand is transferring energy to the imbalance in the head, albeit unconsciously.

Even my ironclad heart couldn't resist the loving energies that seemed to grow daily more intense and inclusive. For the first time in my life I felt the stirrings of love within me. In the energy work sessions, love began to flow through me to the person being treated, and I was opening to the love flowing into me from my fellow students. The workshop, which had begun so painfully, was becoming a series of joyous revelations.

Near the end of our seventeen days, we each had an energy-balancing session with Brugh. When my turn came, he put his hand slightly above my chest, and I felt an absolute waterfall of love pouring into me. Something within me opened to a sublime degree. I felt years of fear and withholding drop away. I was filled to overflowing with this sublime energy. One definition of sublime is "to render finer." I was rendered finer by this transforming experience.

Predictably when I returned to my seemingly less exalted life in L.A., I experienced a thundering crash. All that I had cultivated in the nurturing safety of our desert community vanished, and old patterns of fear and self-protection reappeared. Being in the presence of a gifted teacher can be profoundly heightening. Brugh opened our hearts and ignited love in us all. Now, back in the everyday world, our challenge was to learn to ignite our own hearts, to nurture our own capacity for love. A good teacher discourages dependency. He empowers the student, not himself. Brugh folded up his magical tent and was gone. Now we were on our own.

Following a week of postpartum blues, I had a wonderfully simple dream. In the dream I could see a slight glow all around my body, and I knew it was the glow of loving spirit. I also knew that if I carefully tended this subtle radiance, it would grow and flourish. When I awoke I knew that my heart was *my* responsibility, *my* child, not Brugh's. I knew that with care my heart would prosper.

LOVE

My most vivid movie memory from a youth flooded with films is a haunting scene in Michael Powell's *The Thief of Bagdad,* in which young Sabu, the jungle boy, falls through a vine-covered hole in the jungle floor and tumbles head over heels into a vast cave filled with unbelievable treasure. The glittering cave's prime glory is a golden scepter containing at its top an immense, flashing ruby. The trove is guarded by a huge, ancient cobra that hisses warnings but eventually recognizes that Sabu is pure of heart and befriends the boy.

Even to this day I'm tantalized, mesmerized by this vision of sparkling treasure. In the past it seemed that the allure of this dazzling vision derived from our culture's belief that an abundance of material wealth can solve all our problems and bring endless happiness. But the memory of all those fabulous jewels and piles of golden coins has remained so vivid and resonant within me that I'm certain it carries a deeper personal significance.

The treasure hidden beneath the teeming chaos of the jungle of our world is like the divine inner truth of our being. The scepter's magnificent ruby is our heart, the center of sacred love. This is the treasure of love within the radiant Christ, within the blissful detachment of Buddha. I think the only map to our conscious discovery of this treasure is awareness itself. I suspect the clarity of awareness, the eye of the soul, awakens in us when we tire of and step beyond our preprogrammed, conditioned reactions to life—when we're psychologically and spiritually free of our past.

We're talking about the all-pervasiveness of divine love here. There are of course many other aspects of love.

Our culture focuses overwhelmingly on romantic-sexual love, which, though immensely exciting, thrilling, temporarily transforming, and great fun, is exceedingly conditional and dependent for its very existence on pleasure. Once your lover stops giving you what you want, romantic love is yesterday's newspaper under the litter box. Divine love can pervade romantic love, but I suspect it transforms romance into something quite different from what we're used to seeing and hearing about in movies and pop music.

Then there is our love for our work and our creative endeavors. I love to act and to paint. You might love to teach or to build a business or to nurture a garden or a child.

And there's the unheralded, but profound love of friendship. Romantic love is often most exciting when its object is new, not well known, not familiar, and ripe for conquest. Friendship thrives on time, on knowing its object very well. I suspect that in the long run, friendship partakes of divine love more often and fully than does romance.

It is impossible to comprehend the supreme power, the explosive creativity, the infinite complexity within love's absolute wholeness. Love is the essence of God, of life, of all that is and is not. Love cannot be captured by thought, and yet love is all we are.

The conditioning-shattering, heart-stopping, amazing truth about divine love is that in all its sublime magnificence it is absolutely, totally free. Like sunlight, like the air, love is within and around each of us at all times without any exceptions or conditions whatever. We have only to open our awareness to it to know that love is already here. There is no distance between us and love, ever.

MARTIN

Little did I know that shortly after glimpsing the blissful heights of impersonal love in Brugh's workshop, I would bump smack into a personal love relationship that would last twenty-six years and counting.

Our work with Brugh Joy centered on the divine, unconditional, impersonal aspects of love—what I call love the *noun*. Love, the noun, isn't primarily something you do, it's something you *are*, a state of being. When you open to this level of love, you radiate love in all directions simply because that's what you are.

Personal love is more a verb, an activity, a choice, something you *do*. Divine love has no object, it just *is*. Personal love is an emotion directed from you to a particular someone else or something else. Divine love shines freely like the sun on everything. Personal love tends to be selective and highly conditional. Of course personal love, the verb, can be enriched, indeed transformed by unconditional love.

Not long after the revelations of the workshop I was asked to play the challenging role of Shannon in Tennessee Williams's *The Night of the Iguana* at the Ahmanson Theatre in Los Angeles, directed by my good friend Joseph Hardy. The cast was first-rate: Dorothy McGuire as Hannah, Eleanor Parker as Maxine, and my dearly loved Raymond Massey playing Grandfather in what was to be the final performance of his long and remarkable career.

At our first read-through I met a talented young fellow named Martin who was part of the production team. During the run in L.A. we became friends. As usually happens in show business our acting company split up at the end of our six-week run and everyone, including Martin, leapt off in various directions to distant jobs.

Less than a year later, however, the Circle in the Square Theatre in New York reassembled our *Iguana* production and brought us to Broadway. Martin was promoted to understudy several roles as well as to assistant stage manager, and our friendship picked up where we'd left off. It soon blossomed into romance. In the blissful delirium of our first months together we had no idea of the complex and sometimes arduous destiny we were creating for each other. When the early fires of romance start to ebb, the serious work begins.

If our life is described as a journey from self-centered ignorance and separation toward the wholeness and wisdom of love, then our primary love relationships are life's most rigorous classroom. For those lucky couples who survive the transition from the lovely illusions of hormonal ecstasy into the harsh light of warts-and-all everyday living, life together becomes a workroom (sometimes a war room) of thrilling, scary discoveries; disappointed expectations; painful, glorious realizations; dangerous conflicts; joyous revelations; and ultimately the heady freedom of self-discovery.

Over the years Martin and I have, in between the happy times, fought for control, fought to be *right* (gladly making the other wrong), pushed each other's buttons, aggravated each other's fears, competed for attention, and encountered humongous misunderstandings and misleading expectations. In the course of all this intermittent conflict we've learned voluminously from each other—we've served each other handsomely, if sometimes unintentionally. Our relationship has developed over time into a profoundly beautiful friendship, a kinship of spirit. In short, we've speeded up each other's evolution toward love.

With Martin I've finally learned that being right is irrelevant and not even fun anymore—only the truth matters. Conditional love (the emotion that depends on getting what we want) is still pleasant, but no-strings love is the real thing. And at Martin's continual insistence, I'm at last taking responsibility for the practical aspects of my life and dealing with troublesome events without procrastination and avoidance. I've begun to trust myself and therefore to trust life, trust of any kind being a marvelous novelty in my experience. Something is happening to me that I never really expected—I'm becoming a grown-up, without losing spontaneity and fun.

Ain't love grand?!

And it keeps getting deeper and better. In the years that followed, Martin and I traveled through Mexico, Central and South America, and Easter Island with a small group led by the same wonderful spiritual teachers, Carolyn Conger and Brugh Joy, with whom Martin had toured China.

We spent most of our time exploring the ancient Mayan, Aztec, and Inca ruins. On our way to the legendary Inca stronghold of Machu Picchu we flew from Lima to Cusco in a chartered military transport plane, all of us sitting along the sides of the unadorned cabin shell like soldiers in an old war movie. No peanuts and no toilet. Several hours later, we landed with our ears ringing from the noisy, unpressurized flight.

Our arrival at Cusco was mystical from the start. This was an enchanted, romantic city floating high in the Peruvian Andes. At our lovely hotel we were greeted with steaming cups of coca leaf tea, a brew of the same leaves from which cocaine is extracted. This exotic concoction was supposed to prevent altitude sickness. We drank buckets of it hoping for some sort of illicit high, which sadly never arrived.

On our second day, we were taken just outside of the city to a vast grassy plain that was dotted with partially submerged ruins. We wandered around entranced by the mysterious beauty of the place.

All at once, I was gripped with the urge to turn toward the center of this immense shrine of past Inca glory. There, right at the center, stood Martin as still as the carved stones. He was looking at me with a love that seemed to span centuries. He shone with a kind of love that knows no limits or boundaries. If I were to imagine an archangel or even Christ gazing upon me, their love could not be more complete. I knew at that moment that if there is such a thing as reincarnation, then Martin and I have been together in various guises for eons. I'm more grateful for Martin's love than for anything else in my lifetime.

Somehow we descended from these heights of spirit and returned to "normal." A few days later we traveled by train to the most famous of Inca cities, Machu Picchu. Having spent a morning exploring the ruins, we decided to take an afternoon climb up the famed mountain obelisk called Wayna Picchu that overlooks the settlement of Machu Picchu. We took along a Walkman with two sets of earphones, and Mozart's *Requiem,* with the idea of viewing a spectacular sunset from one of the holiest shrines of the antediluvian world.

Wayna Picchu is a gigantic sword of granite soaring up toward the heavens like the finger of God pointing toward home. We climbed and climbed up narrow, almost vertical stairs that the ancients had carved into the steep mossy sides. Finally at the very top, we gasped at the splendor of a view that seemed to encompass the entire Inca world of long ago. We propped ourselves against the topmost stones, popped on our earphones, and lost ourselves in the mountains and the music and the clouds.

And lost we must have been. As twilight passed and the sky darkened, we suddenly realized that we were going to have to climb down in the dark. We hadn't thought to bring along flashlights. We each thought silently that we were done for. One slip and we'd be meeting our maker.

In the sheer blackness of night it was a challenge to find each carved step. The Incas were a rather short race and they must have had tiny feet because the steps were very small. Nearest the top of the mountain, the most precarious part of the climb, each step was parallel to the cliff. It was difficult enough to sidestep up this final section of the mountain in the light of day, but in darkness it was madness. We moved down as slowly and as carefully as we could, barely daring to breathe. Then, gradually, a near miracle happened. A tiny light seemed to be moving around my feet. And then there were three of these odd lights. And then four. More and more of these little lights started flashing around us. We were nonplussed. Suddenly, we were surrounded by what seemed like hundreds and hundreds of them. Fireflies. Glorious heaven-sent fireflies. Their little dancing lights gave just enough illumination to guide our way down. We were giddy with delight and relief. Those sweet little bugs probably frequented Wayna Picchu every night during that time of year, but we felt that somehow the angels had a hand in it. Whoever sent them, we thanked every last one of those sparkling, lifesaving little creatures.

In the late 1970s, hot on the heels of *Iguana,* I was asked to do one of director Peter Weir's first films, called *The Last Wave,* in Australia, so we headed off from New York City to new adventure. At the time, Weir was a young filmmaker associated with Australia's new wave of auteurs who were filming authentic Australian stories from a fresh perspective. The Australian film industry until then had mostly recycled American and British fare. *The Last Wave* is often paired with Weir's stunning breakthrough film, *Picnic at Hanging Rock,* which also explored the uneasy cohabitation of Australia's Aborigines and the colonialists who pitched their civilization on the remnants of ancient aboriginal lands. Both films are eerie and mysterious, calling into question our literal Western way of looking at the world.

Martin was to be part of the production team, but Peter needed help writing his next project, *Gallipoli,* and enlisted Martin to do the necessary and fascinating research.

Peter was quite young at the time and resembled a charming, pink-cheeked English choirboy rather than a great movie director. But I had seen *Picnic at Hanging Rock,* a study of the profound and frightening mysteries of the ancient Australian landscape, and I knew his bright exterior masked extraordinary hidden depths—much like my character in his film.

I played David, a Waspy young lawyer who, unbeknownst to himself, had a deep connection to the history and mystical powers of the Aborigines. He became involved, through disturbing dreams and mystical visions, in their apocalyptical predictions of a monstrous tidal wave that would soon engulf and cleanse the corrupt world. These visions terrified David and challenged him to learn to accept and eventually embrace his unique connection to the spiritual, primordial wisdom of these ancient tribes.

One of the most compelling scenes in the film is when Nanjiwarra, the tribal elder, confronts David. He tries to get the lawyer to recognize and claim his latent spiritual abilities—and to find out how much he knows of tribal secrets. The two men face each other, sitting on the floor in an empty slum building in Sydney: the dark-skinned tribal shaman, with long grizzled beard and piercing, bottomless eyes; the white lawyer anxious, with a smooth face and spectacles. As they stare at each other as if across centuries, the aboriginal seer asks the modern man a crucial question: "Who are you?" David is baffled and at first has no answer.

"Who are you?" the shaman repeats. And then again, "Who are you?" And again, "Who are you?" hypnotizing David until he answers truly, from some deep recess in himself, that he is not a man but is in fact a "mulkurul" or magical spirit. David's normal circuits of *thinking* have been circumvented by Nanjiwarra's powerful inquiry, and the clueless lawyer suddenly stumbles into *awareness*. In that moment, David realizes who he really is—not just an ordinary man, but a multidimensional spiritual being.

The Australian movie boom was just entering its first burst of creativity, and our young crew worked with an excited exuberance not often found in the highly professional, but sometimes slightly jaded, productions of Hollywood.

Working with the film's tribal Aborigines was a revelation. Like the early Hawaiians they are tuned into nature in ways modern city folks can't even begin to understand. Young David Gulpilil, one of our main actors, was unusual in that he was hip to city ways and comfortable in our urban world but also could throw off his clothes and survive with skill in the Outback, chasing down animals with little more than his bare hands.

Nanjiwarra Amagula, an older actor of great power in the film, was a genuine tribal elder of simple, astonishing integrity. After about half of his scenes were shot, a festering conflict developed between a bunch of "city" Aborigines and Nanjiwarra's tribal group. The city Aborigines deliberately insulted Nanjiwarra's wife, an act that to Nanjiwarra was intolerable. He met with the film's hotshot young producers and said he and his wife would now have to leave the set and return home.

The producers later told me that even though replacing Nanjiwarra and reshooting his scenes with another actor would bring the film disastrously over budget—perhaps even shutting down the whole production—the power of his personal stature and dignity overwhelmed their objections and they found themselves saying yes, of course you must go. Fortunately some intense diplomacy on the part of Peter and the producers eventually resolved the conflict, and Nanjiwarra was able to stay and finish the picture.

As shooting on *The Last Wave* neared completion, one day at lunch break Martin and I chatted with Peter about where we should travel on our way home. Peter suggested some of his favorite places on the island of Bali, that fabled and as yet unspoiled Indonesian enchantress. We thought, okay, and why not Jakarta and India and Nepal, and while we're at it Europe and Scandinavia? So after the picture was in the can we sent nearly all our luggage back home, packed one carry-on each and took off on a trip around the world.

Bali was magnificent, with ancient stone temples, gray and blackened with age. These sprawling edifices, gorgeously silent and melancholy when empty, were brought to vibrant life by various religious ceremonies replete with colorful costumes, lavish offerings of tropical fruit in bright golden containers, incense, and the gay rhythmic clatter of gamelan music. The Balinese honor the powers of both creation and destruction. They often drape statues of deities with cloth checkered in black and white, representing the interdependence of the light and the dark forces.

One afternoon, as Martin and I walked through endless hillside terraces of lush green rice paddies, a group of chattering children carrying long, flexible bamboo poles wandered by. These adorable kids would flip the sticky tops of their poles to catch dragonflies as they sailed through the air, feats of amazing marksmanship. They hung the captured dragons on belt-strings like fishermen collecting fish. When they'd caught enough they took them home, fried them up, and ate the crispy little critters for dinner.

In India we saw the Taj Mahal by the bluish light of the full moon, as well as the less known "Baby Taj Mahal," which was a miniature marble dwelling just as splendid as its more famous parent. As sometimes happens when traveling in India, we were conned by a fancy shop where we bought a lot of beautifully inlaid marble tabletops, dishes, and boxes that were never shipped. Even mighty American Express couldn't pry our merchandise loose from the grasping hands of those nefarious shopkeepers. We spent several languid days on a houseboat in luscious Kashmir, languid, that is, until we both got sick and then discovered that our rather sinister-looking houseboy was using polluted lake water to fill our water bottle and cook our food.

Nepal was a dream. Kathmandu, not yet overrun by tourists, was beyond exotic, with marvelous palaces and temples and strange, yak-flavored cuisine. Buddhism and Hinduism live here in easy harmony, a lesson for us all. On our first afternoon in the city a curious-looking young man befriended us as we left our hotel and offered to be our guide. He seemed intelligent and quite ingenuous, so we let him take us to his favorite shops and temples. At one point he sold us a chunk of hashish for pennies, but as we couldn't figure out how to smoke or ingest it, we hid it in our room at the inn, a surprise for more adventurous future guests.

After outfitting ourselves from various colorful shops, we trekked the Himalayas for a few arduous and mesmerizing weeks. I remember gazing high into the sky at clouds that would suddenly part and reveal—where only the moon and stars should be—the towering mountaintops of Anapurna and Manchepuchuri.

The barefoot sherpas carrying all of our supplies led us through the dreaded leech forest. We Westerners were covered and protected by long-sleeved shirts and pants tied tight around our hiking boots. We were instructed to smear insect repellent on our hands and faces and all over the tops of our boots in case the dreaded leeches dropped on us from the towering rhododendron trees above us. By the time we emerged, the sherpas all had blood-sucking leeches between their toes. They pulled the fat, slippery creatures off with nonchalance and occasional encouragement from the lighted end of their hand-rolled cigarettes.

One sizzling afternoon, after climbing steeply up and then precipitously down a mountainside, we found an inviting river where we stopped to swim in its chilly pools. Drying off in the sun we were suddenly surrounded by clouds of yellow and white butterflies that lit on us and drank the water drops on our skin with their long tongues. It was enchanting to be sipped by these fragile beauties.

Near the end of our trek Martin fell seriously ill with some mysterious malady. On the last day we finally made it to the "end-of-the-trek lodge" where Martin was put to bed with terrible stomach pains and a high fever. A local "medicine man" was called in with only dim results. The next morning as he lay in a virtual coma (later he recalled seeing a circle of vaporous beings surrounding his bed), I went into the breakfast room of our austere mountain "lodge" and found it empty except for two stout middle-aged British women seated several tables away in a corner. They'd heard about my sick friend and asked if I knew the preventive medicine for all such ills. Eagerly I asked what it was. The two lifted their tinkling glasses and said with woozy enthusiasm, "GIN! Darling, lots of GIN!"

With care, we returned to Kathmandu and proceeded to the only hospital in the village, hoping to find a cure for Martin's illness. What we found was exceedingly grim. The female medical worker ushered us into a large rustic room full of patients on wooden tables who were being treated for various illnesses. The scene looked barbaric. She opened a drawer that had several pieces of syringes rolling around like marbles and proceeded to pick out what looked to be the cleanest of the loose needles and other syringe parts. As she started to assemble the contraption and prepared to take a blood sample she nonchalantly asked Martin to offer up a stool sample in an ordinary clay pot like the ones we use for plants. Not quite out of his delirium he looked at me with horror as another worker led him to a greasy cloth that separated the "clinic" room from the toilet. The toilet consisted of a slippery mud floor with a hole in the ground that was filled to the brim with amber-colored liquid. There were two paper cutouts of feet on the mud where one was to squat to do one's business. The stench was enough to send any Westerner fleeing. Martin fled. Fortunately, we were able to catch a plane to Delhi that same day and were in the good hands of a Sikh doctor by nightfall. Copious antibiotics and then boiled foods for six months was the prescribed regimen.

We may not have thought to venture into Africa if it weren't for our friends Jock and Betty Leslie-Melville who lived part-time in Kenya and were intensely involved in animal preservation there. We had an open invitation to visit them and help with their current project: saving the Rothschild giraffes from extinction. We phoned them from Nepal and they said come on over.

Jock and Betty lived in a handsome old stone colonial manse outside of Nairobi. Two "pets"—young Rothschild giraffes—cavorted around their extensive property. One of these majestic animals, Daisy, was made famous by a charming book Betty wrote about her to help finance their animal protection work. Daisy would sometimes lean down and give you a kiss if you approached her with a piece of carrot in your mouth. Martin bravely did this and said the smooch was rather French and sexy.

The five horned Rothschild giraffes were vulnerable to illegal poaching as well as encroaching villages and farms. Jock and Betty had promoted and organized the transfer of these rare animals to a vast national park where they'd have room to thrive. We went along and watched the dangerously tricky operation of rounding up and loading wild giraffes onto trucks that would carry them to their new home. For weeks prior to our arrival they had been fed in the back of the truck beds of several disguised trucks so the animals were accustomed to them. The trick was to lure these beautiful giraffes to their prickly meal of acacia branches while anticipating the wranglers' signal to quickly uncover the truck gate and enclose them. Giraffes are lethal fighters—the flick of a hoof can kill just about anything—so they have to be coaxed along with great skill and care. Thanks to Jock and Betty this complex forced migration was a success, and the Rothschild giraffe continues to flourish in Kenya.

The Melvilles took us on camera safari through a game reserve teeming with wildlife. Once we stopped our open jeep to photograph a couple of rhinos grazing up ahead. Suddenly a lounging lion not six feet away from us lifted its huge head from the tall grass and roared with such awesome power that our vehicle shook and rattled. It scared the daylights out of us, but Martin kept his wits and managed to get a great photo of the beast.

Years later in the mid-1980s Martin and I returned to Africa to act in two films in Zimbabwe—a tongue-in-cheek remake of *King Solomon's Mines* and its sequel, *Allan Quartermain and the Lost City of Gold*. We worked for eight and a half months in the fantastic countryside around Harare, and then we shot at the unbelievable Victoria Falls where the Zambezi River cascades over towering cliffs like a hundred Niagaras. At night during a full moon one can see an extraordinary moonbow over the falls.

Filming these two comic epics was at times a waiting game, hanging around the set while the assistant directors set up huge action sequences with thousands of extras—and at times savage crocodiles! Once in a while I amused myself during these interludes by writing loosely constructed haikus:

Surprised by joy
a mockingbird
cracked the night with song.

Opalescent tide:
quieter
than silence.

Our love
like raindrops splashing:
endless circles.

Wind rustled leaves,
dancing, dancing,
till autumn.

We were spellbound by this dark and magnificent continent for eight and a half months. One of the more amusing moments in our African adventure was a balloon ride over the vast plain of the Masai Mara in Kenya. Being in a balloon afforded us the possibility of viewing the wild animals without their notice, for our human scent would be undetected from the air. The basket under the bright yellow balloon held twelve lucky participants, all eager to photograph the young lion cubs of spring that had been reported to inhabit the area. Once airborne, I removed my dark glasses and hat to facilitate my own picture taking. Unfortunately, this caused a stir among the passengers. Instead of filming the traipsing giraffes, scavenging hyenas, and languid lion dens below, *I* became the caged animal of the moment. It must have been hilarious from the animals' viewpoint to see this balloon basket rocking in the air, as tourists jostled for position to photograph not them but Father Ralph!

We were grateful that we were able to see Bali, Nepal, and parts of Africa before their ancient splendors were gobbled up by the voracious mechanics of our modern world.

For the ultimate in culture shock, our next stop after the heady exotica of Africa and the Orient was the cool, clean decorum of Finland. Martin had spent a year as a high school exchange student in Finland with a wonderful family named Gulin. Martin's family life before his visit had been difficult, and his experiences with the Gulins were like awakening from a troubling dream to the sunshine of uncomplicated affection, harmony, and fun. Martin has an affinity for languages and learned Finnish within a couple of months. After almost a year of this newfound family bliss, he foolishly wrote to his parents in Hawaii saying that he wanted to stay with the Gulins forever. By return mail he received a one-way airline ticket and the order to return home immediately. With a heavy heart he did. When the Gulins tearfully saw Martin off at the airport, his Finnish mother said he'd always be welcome, but if he ever returned it would be wise not to expect everything to be just the same.

But when we arrived at the Gulins' so many years later, everything *was* the same. The whole family happily gathered around Martin as if he'd never left. Juhani, the head of the family, said, "We welcome our son home." The Finns are a very shy people, but once you are admitted into their hearts you are a part of them forever.

Summer in Finland is a revelation of endless daylight. Late at "night" the sun dips briefly below the horizon, only to bob up again and begin its twenty-three-hour day. Filmmakers long to shoot outdoor scenes in the magical, golden, long-shadowed light that precedes sunset, but in most areas those gorgeous moments last only about twenty minutes—hardly time to set up the cameras. In the Finnish summer this golden light lasts for hours.

The sauna is almost a religion in Finland—every home has one. And many families, including the Gulins, have small mountain cabins on the country's more than sixty thousand lakes. These cabins usually have a detached sauna right on the water so you can cook yourself in the extreme heat, make a naked dash into the freezing lake, and then race back to the sauna. A few rounds of this, perhaps with an excellent Finnish beer or two, and you're so relaxed you can barely stand.

Curiously enough, I had a "second family" not unlike Martin's. Now that I'd met the wonderful Gulins, I wanted Martin to meet my wonderful Harveys in England. So off we flew to London.

I had met Eric Harvey, a retired wine and spirits salesman then in his early sixties, on the *Kildare* set at MGM Studios in 1963. We had mutual friends in Los Angeles who introduced us, and Eric, a man of tremendous curiosity and British charm, was fascinated by all aspects of moviemaking. We chatted often on the set for two or three days, and when Eric departed for home, he left a note inviting me to spend the coming Christmas with him and his family in Beckenham. At this point in my life I had never been abroad. I liked Eric and had heard glowing accounts of his wife and kids, so I leapt at this chance to broaden my horizons.

MGM paid for my first-class ticket, and a week before Christmas I flew off into a wonderful adventure. *Kildare* was very popular in England so I took along various disguises and started growing a beard in an attempt to arrive incognito. The attention of media and fans might complicate my brief visit.

As we settled into our seats on the plane the stewardess who served me the mandatory orange juice whispered in my ear that I was sitting across the aisle from the Duke and Duchess of Bedford who were returning home to their immense palace, Woburn Abbey.

Midflight, the duchess, an elegant French woman and the duke's second wife, came over to me and introduced herself. Apparently my disguise wasn't working. She commented on my new beard, saying it was quite attractive, and to my surprise she invited me to come visit them at Woburn. I said I'd love to, never thinking it would really happen.

Eric Harvey picked me up at Heathrow airport and, at his modest home, introduced me to his wife, Cecil, and their three children. I was a bit nervous and staggering from jet lag, but I could see right away that we were all going to get along, although the daughter, Margie, found my American ways and accent very odd and rather funny.

The next day Cecil and Eric were discussing all the places they wanted to show me in their ancient land, and they mentioned that Woburn Abbey was high on their list. I told them about meeting the duke and duchess on the plane and they were thrilled.

A few days later we did visit Woburn with the Harveys' friends the Paddons, and their children and dog, all ten of us piled into a vintage VW camper. Upon arriving, Eric felt it would be rude not to tell the gatekeeper that I had entered the estate.

We drove around the vast grounds awhile and then stopped and set up our picnic lunch under a grand oak tree. As we were eating, a butler drove up in a small car and invited us to afternoon tea at the palace. We warned him that we were ten, eleven with the dog, but he said not to worry, there was plenty of room in the great house for us all.

Everyone but me called the duchess Your Grace (although I was dazzled, as an American I found it difficult at first to kowtow to aristocracy). She met us and gave us a personal tour of her legendary abbey and then led us to a vast but comfortable sitting room and introduced us to the *first* duchess, who had returned to spend the Christmas holidays with her children. With *two* wives in residence for the holidays, the duke had understandably taken to his bed with an undisclosed malady.

Several other family members were present. I remember a young lord holding his two-year-old son. The child already had the haughty bearing of an aristocrat and observed us intruders with disdain. The others were quite charming and friendly. Halfway through our tea several young Bedfords danced into the sitting room spattered with mud from go-carting on the palace grounds. They managed to look glam and chic despite their mud and disarray.

Among the rather casually displayed treasures in the room were two excellent Rembrandt portraits tucked shyly behind other objects. And the huge dining room was hung with perhaps a dozen superb Canalettos so precisely lighted by tiny spotlights hidden in the ceiling moldings that these priceless paintings looked like photo transparencies. The duchess told us with a slight smile that on a recent visit Queen Elizabeth had grudgingly admired this fabulous collection as "better than hers" at Buckingham Palace.

When we reluctantly took our leave from this rarefied tea party, Her Grace the Duchess (I finally caught on) escorted the ten of us (doggie had been entertained downstairs) outside the grandiose front doors. It was twilight. As the duchess told us how delighted she was to have met us all, Nicky, the Harveys' eldest boy, stepped toward her out of the descending darkness and said with the cheeky candor of youth, "Yes, but if it hadn't been for Richard we wouldn't have been invited, would we?" After the tiniest of pauses the duchess cheerfully replied that the Harveys and Paddons would always be welcome at Woburn. The lady had class.

I've been dining out on this story ever since.

Eric Harvey was considerably older than Cecil, and in his previous marriage had fathered a son he dearly loved. The son had died tragically of cancer when he was about my age. I felt that Eric transferred some of his love for his deceased son to me, and I tremendously enjoyed his fatherly affection and advice.

Cecil was an absolute gem, bright, loquacious, great fun, subtly sexy, and a wonderful mom. Along with her wit and exuberant humor, her prime attribute was her innate goodness. She did good things for people not to gain their love and approval, not to win entrée into heaven and outsmart hell, not to please her God. Cecil did good for no reason at all, just because she *was* good. Goodness and virtue are non-transactional; they aren't bargaining chips, nor are they in any way related to reward and punishment.

We all remained close friends, family really, for decades. I've watched their three children grow up, marry, have children, and succeed in business. Cecil was proud of them all and loved being principal baby-sitter at their various homes.

Eric died first, about twenty years ago, and I missed him more than I did my own father when he passed away. Some years later Cecil, who had always seemed robustly happy and healthy, surprised everyone by succumbing to cancer at the too young age of seventy-three. At Christmastime and when I visit England, I still anticipate the warmth of their presence and can hardly believe they're gone.

Though our romp around the fabulous world was as much fun as it was enlightening, flying back home to the excitement of New York was a welcome respite. Martin's Finnish father, the lead pilot for Finnair, flew us home, and allowed us to sit in the cockpit of the spanking new 747 for the landing. We were like little kids earning our junior pilots' wings. When Juhani touched that massive machine down on the tarmac, his piloting skill made it feel like a piece of goose down had just descended to the earth from the heavens.

Travel, with all its pleasures, is hard work. Upon reentry into the Big Apple we relocated to a great apartment on the East Side looking right down Beekman Place. If you leaned way out the living room window, you could see the East River. We even had a working fireplace. It was wonderful finally to have our own home. It wasn't long, however, before I received an offer that would severely strain our still new partnership.

THE FIRST MINISERIES

My agent, Flo Allen, called and said NBC was planning a mammoth twenty-five-hour miniseries dramatizing James Michener's bestselling historical novel *Centennial*, which described America's tumultuous early westward expansion. They wanted me to play Alexander McKeag, a Scots trapper who would dominate the first four hours. McKeag was a hardy, capable fellow who combined masculine prowess with a degree of sensitivity unusual on the frontier. The huge production was to be shot pretty much on location around the actual Platte River in Colorado, a far piece from New York.

I dreaded telling Martin about the job because it would mean leaving our home for months just when we were really getting close. And as I'd guessed, Martin was dead set against my going.

I agonized over the decision, but in my gut I knew I had to go. At that time I *was* my career, my career was *me*. It wasn't clear to me then, but looking back I can see that nothing could stand between me and a great job. Without my work, which I had always felt was a kind of destiny, I simply wouldn't exist.

Young Martin felt abandoned and hurt, but he didn't bolt as I feared he might. When I returned home months later, he was there. Luckily, in New York he had his own career to pursue.

It's my guess that underlying many highly successful careers is a kind of focused mania, a whisper of madness that requires constant achievement to stabilize severe inner imbalance.

At Pomona College, a professor of medieval art once interrupted his lecture to deliver this incisive pronouncement. Referring to the world's most renowned artists, he warned us never to wish to be great. Greatness, he said, results from such severe emotional and mental distress that the artist has no choice but to achieve extraordinary creativity in order to balance his precarious inner anguish and remain sane.

I am certainly no Picasso, but I balanced the dark forces of my fears with the bright lights of creativity and success in a similar way. My career was ninety percent of my identity, leaving about ten percent of me for the rest of my life. By sailing off to do *Centennial,* I quite willingly jeopardized a relationship that was destined to enrich my entire life. And yet, given my love of acting and my intensely neurotic need for continual success and celebrity, I'm not sure I could have chosen differently.

Michener was not known for being terse. His novel covered nearly the entire sweep of American history. It began with the early frontier stories, and my character of McKeag advanced from young manhood to ripe old age in the first four hours. Near the end of shooting the fourth hour my fellow actors Robert Conrad and the beautiful Barbara Carrera, who played my one love, Clay Basket, began to be replaced by new stories and younger characters. We sort of faded from the future just like aging folks in real life. It was a bit eerie to feel the production continuing on without us, leaving us behind.

For a good deal of the shoot we were stationed in the town of Greeley, Colorado, which was convenient for both the river and the plains scenes, and for mountain locations. Along with its country charm, Greeley had one worrisome problem: It was situated between two of America's largest stockyards. No matter which way the wind blew, the place stank. I asked some of the locals how long it would take to get used to the overpowering bovine aromas and they said, "Oh, a couple of years, maybe."

One day on location I was sitting around in my trailer waiting to work when something peculiar happened, peculiar and unnerving. The assistant director knocked on my door and said with barely disguised trepidation that the local police would like to talk with me. I opened the door and in climbed two serious-looking, badged officers carrying what looked like briefcases full of evidence. I asked them to sit down, which they did, one facing me and the other behind me. The cop facing me had a beer-and-burgers belly, a Buffalo Bill mustache, and beady black snake eyes. The one behind was thin, wiry, and deadly serious. I instantly felt like a very guilty suspect on *Law and Order*. Without telling me why, the officer facing me asked with considerable intensity (just like *Law and Order*) where I had been and what I had been doing on several nights the past week. I answered with as much casual charm as I could, considering my ever-deepening guilt. What the officer was doing behind me I did not know—probably preparing to shoot me if I drew a knife or a hidden pistol from my surreptitious ankle holster. Apparently my shaky answers to their probes jibed with information they had already garnered from my fellow workers because the guy behind me stashed his weapon and came around front. They both lightened up and became almost chummy. It seems they thought I might have been the local serial rapist who had killed several young women in the vicinity. The victim the previous night had survived and gave the police a vivid description of her assailant. The resulting police drawing, which they pulled from one of their briefcases, looked exactly like a fan photo of *me* from *Dr. Kildare* days. I was dumbfounded.

As it turned out, playing McKeag was a joy and one of my best performances. I loved the guy, probably because he had all the inner qualities I lacked. He was an anomaly on the rough-and-tumble frontier—he was tough, strong, and capable but also sensitive and kind. He was whole and humane. McKeag needed celebrity like a moose needs a hat rack.

Far more than a number of heroic characters I've played over the years, McKeag, without even knowing it, so trusted himself and life that he was comfortable being that rare creature: a humble nobody. And unlike the actor playing him, he was unafraid of the inner silence and vibrant emptiness that informed his soul.

Folks like McKeag seem to have been born whole, with body, mind, and spirit happily integrated, ready to live their lives fully and well. And then there are the rest of us who were either born somewhat broken and in need of considerable fixing or damaged along the way.

Being one of those in need of a fix, playing the sturdy character of McKeag for several months was a revelation. Every day of shooting *Centennial* I got to actually experience *being* this extraordinarily together man who could negotiate life's roughest waters while remaining kind, warm, and loving; a man to whom self-doubt was unknown, who had no need of accolades or external validation of any kind. Playing McKeag, I felt the confidence and wholeness I'd always dreamed of.

Western culture seems to divide us; one part is our individual search for survival and happiness in the competitive world and the other is the possibility of attaining an "inner" life of spirit. Usually we give the lion's share of importance to the former, viewing the idea of an inner life with suspicion, fearing any hint of self-indulgence or non-Western hocus-pocus. And yet, I suspect our mysterious inner realms of silence and seeming emptiness, however threatening they are to our controlling ego, are in fact the actual source of our life, intelligence, and creativity.

There have been great mystics who believe that this duality is an inevitable source of conflict in our lives and that we must learn to transcend it by ascending in consciousness into full realization of the oneness of all. For a time, attaining this sense of total unity was my goal. It seemed that I had to choose between the hurly-burly of my daily existence and some blissfully detached realm of divine awareness.

I now think that for most of us duality is our lot in life. But I think the chasm between outer and inner, between the seen and the unseen, can be happily bridged by a kind of conscious marriage of body and soul, a wedding of the two like the marriage of male and female or yin and yang. This marriage is not one of convenience, no shotguns needed. It is a love match. A loving mutual interest can unite our temporal lives with the eternal life of spirit, the life of spirit being a kind of communion with and participation in something much greater than ourselves.

While playing the role of McKeag, I felt this holy union was complete within him, unconsciously. Having had this experience of wholeness vicariously through McKeag, I am eager to nurture with loving attention this holy matrimony within myself. As in the marriage of two people, each must relinquish dominance and control in favor of cocreating a life together.

FATHERS AND SONS

My all-time favorite job was a new play by Tom Babe called *Fathers and Sons*, which was staged at the Public Theatre in New York City. At the center of the story was an aging Wild Bill Hickok, holed up, back against the wall in a run-down saloon out west. Wild Bill passed his time playing poker and boozing and romancing Calamity Jane until his bastard son appeared, hankering to shoot his infamous father to gain revenge and his own few minutes of fame.

Our director, Robert Allan Ackerman, cast me as Bill, the stupendous Dixie Carter as Jane, and a marvelous bunch of cowboy actors we all recognized from old B-movie westerns.

Dixie and I sparked together from the very first, and we had an electric chemistry onstage. Along with her extraordinary talent, Dixie is a classic southern belle, who in a wink can make a man feel brilliant, funny, and sexy all at the same time. I was crazy about her, on- and off-stage.

Tom Babe had a most magical way with language. His colorful exaggerations of western dialogue were sheer delight to speak, lifting his characters into mythic stature. *And* we each had a song.

During rehearsals Tom kept rewriting the end of the play. First I killed my son. Then we tried having my son, who had tied me to a chair on top of the bar, kill me. In the final version we shot each other. During all my theater work this was the only new play I had ever done. It was thrilling to originate a character and to take part in the creation of the play.

A couple of years later we revived *Fathers and Sons* at the intimate Canon Theatre in Beverly Hills, produced by Leslie Moonves, who now runs the CBS network. The venue brought me full circle: When I was a kid, the same theater was called The Hitching Post—and played the B-movie westerns that many of our cast had acted in.

SHOGUN

Like some sort of tidal wave, *Centennial* kicked off a fabulous miniseries ride that surfed me through the 1980s. Of course I had no idea what fate had in store until the roiling waves tumbled me into sixteenth-century Japan.

I first heard the word *Shogun* in my dressing room behind the stage of the Ahmanson Theatre in Los Angeles in the mid-1970s. I was appearing as Cyrano de Bergerac, and out of the small knot of friends who had gathered to wish me well after the show, a tall man with an open smile and piercing eyes stepped forward to ask if I'd read the book. Not only had I not read it, I seemed to be the only person in the country who had not heard of James Clavell's bestselling novel about the shipwrecked British sailor who washes ashore in Japan in 1600 and finds himself in the middle of a great feudal war. The man told me to read *Shogun*, not only because it was a gripping epic tale, but because he thought it would make a terrific miniseries. I would soon come to regard our meeting as fated, for it was through this kind stranger that I found one of my best and most artistically satisfying roles.

I read Clavell's book as if in a trance. I couldn't put it down, captivated not only by the political intrigue of Japan's feuding warlords but also by the classic romantic tragedy of *Shogun:* the forbidden love affair between the Englishman John Blackthorne and his Japanese interpreter, Mariko. The story resonated with me, sparked my own memory of my time in the East. I had been a soldier once, a sergeant in the army after the Korean War. On a visit to Japan, I, too, had taken comfort in the arms of an exotic and beautiful woman, who led me to bed after a fragrant, languid bath in a deep, wood-paneled tub.

As soon as I finished the book, I called my agent, Flo Allen, at the William Morris Agency. I was obsessed with *Shogun,* I told her, and wanted desperately to see it as a miniseries for the small screen. I was born to play the role of the dashing Blackthorne, I said. As agents often do, though, Flo brought me back to reality. I was late in discovering Clavell's book. A movie studio had already snapped up the rights.

"There's another problem," Flo said. "And it has a name: Robert Redford."

I was disappointed by what she told me, but after nearly twenty years in Hollywood, I knew that things could change and often did. I decided to be patient, sure that the expansive, panoramic story of *Shogun* would prove too difficult for a studio to pare down into a two-hour movie for Robert Redford. After several frustrating attempts to come up with a script, the studio grudgingly surrendered the rights to NBC television.

I called Flo again. "Now," I said, "now I can play Blackthorne."

"Fine," she said. "But your problem has a new name: Sean Connery."

Author James Clavell was to have an unusual amount of influence on any production. Not only had *Shogun* sold more than seven million copies since its publication in 1975, but Clavell was also a screenwriter of such movie classics as the original version of *The Fly* with Vincent Price, *The Great Escape,* and *To Sir, With Love.* Along with Eric Bercovici, he was also cowriting the screenplay of *Shogun.* It was Clavell who wanted Connery to play Blackthorne. And, barring that, the author insisted on a British actor for the part. So much for fate.

"Fine," I told Flo. "We'll wait and see."

Sean Connery was soon out of the running for *Shogun,* after he was offered another role in a feature film that paid much more money. Clavell then suggested Albert Finney for the part, but Finney wasn't interested, joking that the massive script "had to be delivered on a dolly." Although there were a lot of other British actors clamoring to play Blackthorne, NBC wanted me. It was the businessmen at the network who persuaded Clavell to meet me.

The author of *Shogun* greeted me that night in the bar of the Beverly Wilshire Hotel, with a firm handshake and an appraising look. We walked to the dining room slowly, Clavell favoring one leg. It was the result, he told me, of a motorcycle accident he'd had in the 1940s. His slight limp coupled with a dueling scar on his cheek gave him the dashing air of a buccaneer. When we were seated at a linen-covered table, Clavell lit his pipe. With smoke curling around him, he began to tell me about himself, a story almost as interesting as the fictional one we were thinking of bringing to television.

The sea was in his blood, he said. Both his father and grandfather were career officers in the British Royal Navy, and Clavell had lived in Hong Kong and other colorful ports of call. Foreign phrases peppered his vocabulary, and, with his British accent, he seemed worldly and sophisticated. It was hard to believe that the elegant, pipe-smoking man sitting across from me had spent three and a half years in Japanese prisoner of war camps, including the notorious Changi Prison near Singapore, where only one in fifteen men survived.

I was so excited during dinner that I hardly ate. I had done my homework; not only had I read Clavell's novel again and again, but I had researched the subject on my own. I knew Clavell had been inspired by the true story of William Adams, a sea captain who, blown off course by storms, became the first Englishman to visit Japan and later established a trade route with the islands. I felt as if I had studied for an important exam, and I was waiting for Clavell to test my knowledge.

I was also sweating. Not from nervousness but from the layers of T-shirts I wore under my shirt and sport jacket. I had sensed what Clavell wanted was not only a good actor but a big, manly actor for his Blackthorne. So, to prepare for this meeting, I did exercises to lower the pitch of my voice. I'd also been spending a lot of time in the gym, working out with weights. I had firmed up significantly, but on the night of our meeting, I still borrowed an old trick that Don Murray used in his role as a cowboy in *Bus Stop:* I wore extra layers under my shirt for a brawnier appearance.

Despite our long, intimate talk, I left that night without the part. Clavell was not convinced. So we arranged to meet again, this time at Clavell's home in Hollywood. I met his charming wife, April, who had once been an aspiring ballerina and actress. Perhaps it was the gentle pressure of his wife, with whom I got along swimmingly, or the not-so-subtle urging of NBC as the shooting deadline approached—I don't know. But the next day, it was Flo who called *me*. Blackthorne was mine.

After all those months of suspense, I was ecstatic. I knew in my bones that this great part in this lush tale would completely redefine my career. Each of *Shogun*'s millions of readers and everyone in Hollywood had an opinion of who should play Blackthorne, but now it was up to me. I knew what an incredible opportunity this was, and I was determined to make it work.

Our first weeks of shooting in Japan were for me an uneasy time of adjustment. Some of the scenes were quite difficult to film, especially the storm sequences that lead to the shipwreck. Full-size replicas of the English ships were built in a giant outdoor tank at Toho Studios outside Tokyo, and for two weeks we acted after dark while the crew sprayed us with cold rain. The ships bobbed and tipped precariously on ancient machinery as huge wave machines transformed the tank into a raging sea. After a few nights of suffering, we actors discovered the medicinal and wonderfully warming effects of Japanese brandy.

But the first of many problems was brewing. The nightly storms that the *Shogun* crew manufactured irritated local residents who lived near the studio. They complained about the constant noise and activity and sent police to stop the production. Only after James Clavell plied our neighbors with cases of sake were we able to finish the scenes.

Clavell appeared on the set every day for the first two weeks. As if the shoot were not challenging enough, I also had to contend with his lingering doubts about my ability to play Blackthorne. I could feel his eyes following me in every scene. I knew I was being evaluated, held up for comparison with someone else he had imagined in the role. I rose to the occasion, however, and used the added scrutiny to bring intensity and focus to my work. Finally, after fourteen torturous days, Clavell decided he liked what he saw and entrusted his beloved Blackthorne to my care. He left Japan for California. And without Clavell's constant presence, I was able to settle into my role.

But *Shogun* ultimately was an arduous experience for everyone involved. The summer turned ferociously hot. I struggled, too, to breathe life into my lines. The script had ballooned to nearly six hundred pages, and I was in almost every scene. Blackthorne's dialogue at times seemed endless and largely expositional. That is, it delivered necessary information to the audience but didn't result from emotional exchanges between characters.

But the biggest problem, and the most disastrous, was the war that exploded almost immediately between the American and Japanese contingents of our crew and production team.

Our large Hollywood crew charged onto *Shogun*'s Tokyo locations like medieval crusaders come to convert the Asians to the American way of filmmaking. Like Blackthorne and his shipmates, the Yanks hadn't bothered to learn about Japanese customs, pride, or their rigidly complex forms of courtesy. Early in the production one of our crew guys yelled in exasperation, "Haven't you fuckers ever made a movie before?" It was a crude insult, unimaginable to the Japanese. The battle lines were drawn, and covert warfare didn't cease until the final days of shooting.

Another mistake was to use female interpreters to transmit director Jerry London's orders to the assistant directors, who were all Japanese men. At that time in Japan it was unheard of for women to have leadership roles in society. Each time the assistant directors were told to do something by the interpreters, they felt as if they were being bossed around by women, and they resented it. As a result, they seemed to screw up purposely as often as possible.

The conflict between the Japanese and American crews grew so acrimonious that the Americans began walking on the near-sacred tatami mats with their shoes on, blasphemous to the Japanese. The tatami mat is never just a prop, even on movie sets. Of course, the Japanese producers were not innocent bystanders in this seething culture clash, bedeviling our production with their unceasing efforts to increase their profits.

And no one bothered to explain to the Yanks that in Japan it was considered impolite to say no, part of their ritualized courtesy and avoidance of confrontation. For Americans, who revere clear thinking and direct attacks on problems, this kind of subtle distinction created a great deal of confusion. You had to listen very carefully to the way in which the Japanese said yes to determine whether they really meant "yes"—or "get lost."

Even the meals on set proved to be a problem. If the food was too "Western," the Japanese crew would complain. But for Americans, a diet heavy in sushi and other exotic fare was often hard to swallow. In the larger cities, more variety was available, but smaller locales meant more local cuisine. "We had squid every day we were there and in every way possible: raw, pickled, broiled, boiled, and fried," remembered producer Eric Bercovici of a shoot in Nagashima.

The American and Japanese crews should have been like two giant wings carrying the same bird, but they weren't. Perhaps the story of *Shogun* itself stirred up some of these atavistic feelings among the Japanese about the English missionaries, the tribal conflicts, and the wickedly complicated history of great nations.

The communication problems and lack of cooperation between the two crews almost resulted in disaster during the filming of the tremendous earthquake scene outside of Kyoto. It was shot in an eerie valley etched with deep, naturally eroded trenches. Our special effects expert, Bob Dawson, covered these trenches with a thick layer of dirt on plywood sheets supported by poles that, when blasted with gunpowder charges, were supposed to cave in, giving the effect of quake fissures splitting the earth and swallowing up samurai, tents, and horses.

Seven cameras were set up to photograph the spectacular event. After meticulous rehearsals, the cameras rolled and the charges exploded but nothing happened; no fissures appeared. Rain the night before had solidified the ground so that it wouldn't cave in.

The company moved to a nearby spot to shoot another scene, while Dawson and three assistants climbed down into the trenches to prepare for a second try at making the earthquake. But just as we were about ready to start filming, we heard cries. One of the trenches had collapsed on Dawson and his men.

It was pandemonium, with Japanese and American crew members yelling and running around. No one seemed to know how to talk to anyone. The crews that by then, very late in the shoot, should have worked like a well-oiled machine, could not even come together during a crisis. Finally, our cinematographer, Andy Lazlo, took charge and came up with a plan to rescue the trapped men. They were freed after an hour of careful digging.

Despite its trials, making *Shogun* was incredibly rewarding. We were given weekends off, which was unusual for a film shooting on location, where production expenses are often much higher and demand a six-day workweek. On Saturdays and Sundays, my beautiful Japanese interpreter Mieko (whom I didn't mind at all taking orders from) would show me around Tokyo or Osaka or Nagashima or, best of all, Kyoto.

Kyoto is a treasure, full of magnificent temples and ancient palaces. Once, Mieko and I explored a nearby mountain called Mount Hiei, which was dotted with hundreds of temples and small shrines. At one of them, we happened upon a sacred drama performed by a large group of

gorgeously costumed monks and priests. Their chanting was punctu-
ated by strange musical interludes with drums and gongs. We weren't
allowed inside the temple, but we could watch and listen through lightly
veiled windows. I was spellbound by these dedicated "actors" who performed with such precision and power. It was like sailing back in time
to see the origins of my own profession, in its earliest incarnation as
purely religious expression.

On another enchanted day, Mieko and I were driving by a mountain lake in Kyoto that was filled with colorful barges and rowboats, all
part of an amazing celebration to mark the annual turning of the leaves.
Exotic Kabuki and No dramas were performed on the various barges.
Mieko and I joined the other observers, skimming across the lake in a
rowboat to watch the different displays. Happily, there was also a barge
passing out free glasses of sake. We were all getting a bit looped as we
rowed through the barge dramas, and there were a number of jovial
boating mishaps. Only the Japanese, an inherently poetic people, could
invent such an extravagantly bizarre and beautiful way to celebrate the
simple change of seasons.

MIFUNE-SAN

S*hogun* gave me the opportunity to collaborate with wonderful Japanese actors. Yoko Shimada won the part of Lady Mariko after an intensive talent search throughout Japan. She was an important star there and crowds gathered just to catch a glimpse of her. In spite of her warrior husband and other dangers, Lady Mariko risks becoming Blackthorne's lover. Yoko played her perfectly, even though she had to act in a foreign language. The story of Blackthorne and Lady Mariko's affair, doomed as it was, was powerful to me. Although surrounded by brutality, Blackthorne is able to keep an open heart, to give and receive love. It was a message that I may not have been so attuned to then but that would later flower in my personal life.

On *Shogun*, I also had the honor of working with Toshiro Mifune, Japan's biggest movie star and arguably one of the greatest actors of all time. As an ardent fan of foreign films of the 1950s, I had seen director Akira Kurosawa's *The Seven Samurai* and *Rashomon,* starring that man-leopard, Mifune. I had been frightened and dazzled by his physical and spiritual power. At our first meeting prior to filming *Shogun,* I approached Mifune-san with awe and caution, but found him unexpectedly reserved and a bit shy. In a blue blazer and gray slacks, Mifune-san pretended to speak little English, but I suspect he understood a great deal.

Mifune, who played Lord Toranaga, was a gentle man off camera. But in costume, particularly as a samurai, he became a force of nature, like a tsunami that rises up out of the sea and imposes its will on every-thing in its path. Before a scene, a savage, low growl would often emanate from Mifune, rumbling from him like distant thunder. Neither I nor anyone else dared to go near him on set, except in the line of duty.

But this great man was full of surprises. One day during our lunch break, he saw me hiding a Japanese coin in the rafters of the set ceiling. Mifune was overcome with laughter, saying I was "pure Japanese," pre-ferring to keep my money under the mattress rather than in a bank. I laughed, too. It was a small but intimate moment in which, however briefly, we both left the veneer of courtesy and discretion behind.

Another time, on an outdoor set, Mifune noticed that my straw sandals were not tied correctly and so he got down on his knees and retied them himself. It was like having your shoes shined by God because status is extremely important to the Japanese—they secure and maintain their position with great care and pride—and at the time of *Shogun* Mifune-san was at the very pinnacle of his career. I was touched by that gesture.

One day, we were shooting a climactic scene in which Toranaga calls together all his various warlords and their armies in preparation for a great battle. The outdoor set was a huge arena, enclosed by a wall of gorgeous cloth banners that surrounded a dais, where Toranaga was to address the warriors. Blackthorne, having become Toranaga's most trusted samurai, was seated on the edge of the dais watching the majes-tic arrival of each army and awaiting the final entrance of Toranaga himself. The long scene was to be shot from a high tower at the far cor-ner of the set. Jerry London, our director, yelled "Action!" and the lords and their armies marched in with tremendous dignity. After the hun-dreds of soldiers were in place, Toranaga was to ride in on horseback, dismount, and approach the dais.

Well, there we were, all in place. And no Toranaga. After what seemed like history's longest pause, I heard the sound of hoofbeats charging unimaginably hard and fast. Then Mifune, who had said earlier that he was rather frightened of horses, shot into the vast arena like lightning, heading straight for the dais and straight for me. He was galloping faster than any stunt man I've ever seen in my life. I thought to myself, "Mifune has lost control of his mighty steed and in about half a second, I'll be trampled to death by the rampaging pair." Then, like pure magic, Mifune and his stampeding horse stopped right on their mark. Almost too quickly to see, Mifune dismounted and was striding toward me, as if he'd just appeared out of thin air. Thank God we didn't have any dialogue until the next shot, because I was literally struck dumb. I felt like madly applauding or just bowing in reverence.

Jerry London's voice boomed from the tower, "Very nice, Toshiro. We're going to shoot it again." I couldn't believe that Jerry would think that this miracle of horsemanship could be repeated, especially since the horses we used in Japan were not specially trained for films. They were practically wild. I had done quite a bit of horseback riding for films, and I knew that a horse galloping flat out like that cannot be stopped so suddenly without pain. I knew the horse would likely balk if made to do it again.

But I guess Jerry hadn't done much riding, because he asked Mifune to repeat this phenomenal equestrian feat not just once but seven times. On the seventh take, the horse inevitably shied, charged around behind the enclosure and threw Mifune-san to the ground. Instead of raging against the director and threatening to sue the production for reckless endangerment, Mifune-san, who had to be hospitalized for observation, was found on the ground, weeping with shame. He felt he had let everyone down. This great and incomparable man sent flowers and notes of apology to the director and the producers and returned to work two days later.

After the disastrous earthquake scene and now Mifune being thrown from his horse, the Japanese began to fear that evil spirits were jinxing the location. The shoot continued to be plagued by so many upsets and near disasters that we brought in a Buddhist priest who blessed the land with sacred sake. He said the special effects team had killed a snake and so had angered the area's *Kami*, or nature spirits. As I watched the priest in his saffron robe lighting incense and chanting prayers, I thought about how courtesy, which is really respect, is due not only to humans, but to the earth and its creatures as well.

My turn at reckless endangerment came near the end of the production. A huge night shoot had been planned to film a crucial scene that involved an armada of small boats filled with Toranaga's men. Led by Blackthorne, they were to attack and destroy the Jesuits' infamous black ship in the harbor. With so many boats, so many samurai, and so many single-shot guns, the logistics of the scene were extremely complicated and precise. Partly because of the tensions between the Japanese and American crews, preparations for this battle scene took most of the night, and the delays were driving Jerry London crazy. We had to shoot the scene before dawn, and dawn was getting ever closer. We were already way over budget, and an extra night's filming, with all these people, would be disastrous.

Jerry and the camera barge were to move freely between all our boats, and I had just one line, one word actually. At precisely the right moment, I was to yell, "Fire!" That would signal my men to shoot their muskets at the dreaded black ship, where all hell would break loose.

Finally, as the sky was beginning to lighten, everything was set and with tremendous anxiety Jerry yelled, "Action!" We started to row like mad toward the towering black ship. Suddenly, I realized I didn't know how the director would signal me to shout my line. I could barely make out the camera barge in the distance and without thinking, I yelled, "Jerry, when do you want me to say, 'Fire'?" Well, all the Japanese soldiers understood was that last unfortunate word and they shot their muskets like maniacs while poor Jerry yelled fruitlessly, "No! No! Stop!"

The shot was ruined, and the inevitable dawn approached. Jerry was pissed off beyond words, but somehow the prop guys got all the guns reloaded, no small task in itself. The boats were reset, and we shot the scene again with special nighttime filters on the cameras. Just seconds before the sun came up, we finally got it right, and my ass was saved from the slings and arrows of outrageous fortune.

Throughout the wonders, rigors, splendors, and daunting challenges of making *Shogun*, a line from a poem I'd always thought was rather silly kept popping into my head: "If you can keep your head while all about you are losing theirs . . ." Or more appropriately, "If you can keep your *wa* [the Japanese word for inner harmony] while all about you are approaching meltdown . . ."

Just about all my eggs, personal and professional, were riding in the *Shogun* basket, and no matter how tough things got, I knew I had to keep an unwavering grip on my *wa* and get that precious basket across the finish line unscathed. Thanks to Jerry London, Eric Bercovici, Andy Lazlo, our mostly terrific crew, and wonderful actors, we did just that.

During the shooting of *Shogun* (six and a half months on location), I was often just too busy to pay much attention to my personal development. And yet I do vividly remember two simple but powerful experiences.

One weekend afternoon I was idly wandering the streets of Kyoto when I passed a small temple in a tree-filled park. Autumn leaves danced down in a soft breeze. The park was empty except for a lone Japanese woman sweeping the falling leaves from otherwise immaculate grounds. She was slight, slender, straight-backed, about fifty, and she performed her almost ritual movements with a profound, utterly simple dignity. Casually viewed, her humble task could seem barely relevant, and yet I had the feeling that she carried the presence of a guardian spirit committed in the most holy way to the care of the ancient temple and the sacredness it contained. I realized as I watched for just a few moments that this tiny woman was no less a personage than the emperor.

On another day several friends and I visited a magnificent Shinto temple complex in the wooded hills outside of Kyoto. Many magnificent shrines and temples were set among gardens and koi ponds filled with water lilies and flowering lotus. As we strolled along, mesmerized by the beauty of the place, I noticed an intense, middle-aged Japanese woman bowing reverently at several different shrines.

As we approached the main temple, a huge wooden structure gorgeous in its simplicity, we were disappointed to see that its inner sanctum was shrouded from sight by carefully hung curtains protecting its inner holiness from casual view. Again the frail Japanese woman was kneeling before the temple with almost heartbreaking reverence.

Then, as we observed her in total, motionless silence, the most extraordinary thing happened. As if moved by the praying woman's devotion, a sudden breeze gently blew open the curtains revealing the sacred altar within. It was as if somehow her prayers were answered. In that exquisite moment, before our very eyes, she had been touched by grace.

On September 15, 1980, the first installment of *Shogun* aired, and half of all televisions in America were tuned to it. Even our gutsy gamble to have long passages of Japanese dialogue spoken without subtitles had paid off. Rather than be confused by it, as NBC had feared, the audience seemed to understand that the Japanese was designed to create the same state of mystification that Blackthorne and his crew found themselves in upon landing in Japan.

Shogun was a stupendous success all over the world. The five-night, twelve-hour "maxiseries" became a phenomenon. It did wonders for sushi bars, popularizing the delicacy in America. On the nightly news after each broadcast, reports showed packed Benihana steak houses where people had gathered to watch the show. Newspapers published long plot summaries and "glossaries" of Japanese phrases and words. T-shirts with the Japanese flag on them and decorative samurai swords were flying off the shelves. Even the National Educational Association endorsed *Shogun,* recommending it to American students as "a culturally broadening adventure story." Ultimately, about 130 million people saw at least part of the series.

Shogun was a godsend to me. I was again in love with my career and my celebrity life. In the end, all the conflicts and difficulties of the shoot were forgotten.

The success of the show also moved me to the head of the class of actors being considered for the role of Father Ralph in another upcoming miniseries that NBC was planning—*The Thorn Birds*. Except for one little problem: The studio wanted Robert Redford.

NANA

Three years before *Shogun,* Martin and I were visiting his family in Hawaii. He had grown up there, we had always dreamed of living by the sea, and we were looking for a beach house we could afford. We lucked out and found a great little house on Oahu, out in the country where the locals live. It sits on a point facing west toward the sunset and the lofty Waianae Mountains, and the view is unsurpassable.

While I was filming *Shogun* in Japan in 1979, Martin was traveling through China with a spiritual group led by Brugh Joy and Carolyn Conger. The group returned to the U.S. mainland via Hawaii. I'd just arrived at our island home, and we spent a few days together on Oahu where we were joined on several occasions by Brugh's friend and fellow teacher Nana Veary, otherwise known as Nana.

Nana was a descendant of the old Hawaiian aristocracy. She was born on the island of Oahu in 1908 and raised by her Hawaiian elders in a now vanishing world, where fishing, healing, building, and all aspects of their lives were done in total communion with nature. It was an island world where children planted by the moon and strangers were greeted with reverence. Birds, clouds, rainbows, and stones spoke as clearly as people—a "silent language" of the earth. Their entire world, if listened to, was full of wisdom.

Nana grew up surrounded by spiritually aware people. Her mother, Mary, was a gifted healer, letting the forest plants and herbs tell her what was needed to treat various illnesses. When fishing, Mary would chant and pat the seawater, inviting the fish to come to her and nourish her family. They did. She took only what she needed.

Nana's spiritual journey started early and with total dedication. Ancient Hawaiian influences intertwined with her mother's Christianity—a fertile combination. On her continuing quest, Nana was baptized into the Pentecostal Church where she learned an unshakable faith and love for the Spirit of God within herself. She was a spiritual medium for a while. Then she studied metaphysics with Ernest Holmes, the founder of the Church of Religious Science in Los Angeles, and later enjoyed a deep association with the late Zen master Tanouye Tenshin.

Nana's magnificent spirit distilled these various and complex teachings into a potent elixir of pure simplicity. She opened herself unreservedly to the presence of God within her and wholeheartedly dedicated herself to sharing this divine loving intelligence with everyone she met. In Nana's book *Change We Must* she said, "The consciousness of God in the human soul is the essence, the sum and substance of all religion. It is the essence of the teachings of all the seers and mystics in the world's history. To become centered in God Consciousness is the first essential of every satisfactory life. The second is to go out thinking, speaking, working, loving, and living from this center to serve God in others. Service is the greatest principle of practical ethics."

Nana became our dear friend here in the islands. She was great fun socially and was wonderfully informative about island lore. She loved to tell stories of how the jungle birds told her father, a master canoe builder, which termite-free trees he should use for his canoes. Her mother, she said, swam with and even rode on a particular shark that was her *aumakua*, her personal guardian spirit. And she held numerous silent retreats for various groups at our beach house on Oahu, as well as in the high mountains of Koke'e, Kauai, which she loved for its beauty and vibrant quiet.

In *Change We Must*, Nana writes about the practice of meditation that is fundamental to her silent retreats:

In meditation, after a period of contemplation, we rise in consciousness into an atmosphere of receptivity, into a consciousness where miracles take place. We come to a place of transition where Truth leaves the mind and enters the heart. Truth is no longer an intellectual knowledge about "Truth," but rather a living thing within our own being. With a change of consciousness, we *are* Truth.

Here Nana is referring to the difference between verbal thinking (our thinking is always verbal and consequently abstract) and "awareness," which is our ability to see and understand something immediately, directly, and wholly beyond the conceptualization of thought, beyond words.

It's important to understand the difference between thinking and awareness. Thinking is always conceptual, rather than concrete. The idea of a horse is not a horse, the idea of love is not love. Thinking, however useful, is always abstract and at a distance from the thing thought about.

Awareness, on the other hand, needs no words or concepts. Awareness is direct knowing. When we are aware of the horse or of love, we actually share our being with the horse or with love. Awareness is not "about" love, awareness is an intimate rapport with love. Through the communion of awareness, Nana and truth became one.

In the early seventies a friend who had recently introduced a group of friends to Japanese food, raw fish, and sushi (which were fairly exotic back then) also encouraged us to try Transcendental Meditation. If he was right about sashimi, he might be right about meditation, so we dutifully enrolled. This form of meditation was made famous when the Beatles adopted its teacher, Maharishi Mahesh Yogi, as their spiritual guru.

Introductory TM is a very simple method taught by TM centers throughout the world. Our little group went to the meetings together, and we "graduated" in a sunset ceremony where we offered fruit to the memory of the great TM masters of the past.

We were taught to sit comfortably in a quiet room, close our eyes, and to be very aware of our breathing while watching our thoughts as we might watch clouds coming and going in the sky. We were each given a mantra, a simple Sanskrit word to repeat in our mind to quiet our thinking. The purpose was to calm our active mind's chatter and to de-stress. The deeper purpose was to tap into the inner silence of our being.

In the beginning classes, I felt foolish sitting there breathing and silently repeating the musical mantra. I was embarrassed by the blabber of my thinking since I expected some sort of sublime experience. But over the years I began to gently reap the rewards of this ancient practice. I have found the experience rich and peaceful and have occasionally been touched by insight. I no longer repeat my mantra, that lovely word, whose meaning I never knew.

Every meditation is different, but I usually begin by giving my entire attention to my heart area, the physical seat of love. More often than not, my heart responds with a feeling of radiant, loving energy that seems to open my mind to some degree of wholeness. I'm not sure I've ever touched the complete inner silence Nana spoke about. My sense of self is not yet willing to die into nothing (or everything) even for a few moments.

In Hawaii, it's considered wise to have your home (or new office or new project) blessed in the ancient manner, so we asked Nana to bless our beach house. She came for dinner the evening before and stayed the night.

The next morning before dawn we followed as Nana sprinkled salt-water from a koa bowl with a long ti leaf and solemnly chanted the sacred sayings. As we entered a small upstairs bedroom, she stopped at the door and stared at an old rocking chair in the corner. She spoke to the chair in Hawaiian, listened a moment, and then laughed delightedly.

Later she explained that she had seen our house ghost sitting in the rocker (just about everyone but me had seen this female ghost at one time or another). She had asked the ghost who she was and what she was doing there, and the ghost had replied with considerable attitude, "So what's with *you*?"

As the sun rose outside Nana chanted to the dimming moon and to the sea and then to the rising sun, and we sensed that they all heard her and responded. Later Nana released the ghost back to the "place of learning," and no one saw our incorporeal friend again.

Some months later Martin asked Nana to give him a Hawaiian name. Again she spent the night at our beach house. By morning the spirits had told her Martin's name: Moanikealaonakoolau, which means "the gentle morning mist that carries the scent of the blossoms over the Koolau mountains." Nana then cooked Martin a whole *kumu* (fish once eaten only by Hawaiian royalty) wrapped in a ti leaf and told him to eat every bit of flesh. When he finished, she rewrapped the head and bones in the ti leaf and flung the package into the sea on the crest of a small wave. If the wave took it back out to sea, it would mean the correct name had been chosen. The ti leaf and bones drifted away out of sight.

A year later I asked Nana what my Hawaiian name might be. She closed her eyes a moment, then said it was Nohea. And what does Nohea mean, I asked, hoping for something the poetic equal to Martin's. "Handsome," she said without ceremony. No fish, no ti leaf, no scented morning mist. I disguised my disappointment with smiling thanks. That evening my spirits lifted a bit when I looked up "handsome" and was reminded that along with "good looking" it also meant "generous."

Once, early in our friendship, Nana invited me to breakfast with her at her favorite restaurant, Michelle's. I was delighted to join her, but I had never been alone with her and I was quite nervous. I was in awe of Nana and found myself trying to be as bright and amusing and "deep" as possible. Every quiet moment in our conversation seemed scary (I felt I was somehow letting her down), so I chattered on like an endless TV commercial. Nana said less and less.

As I drove Nana to her home, she was thoughtful and silent. In her driveway I opened the car door for her. She stood up and faced me for a long moment with a look of seriousness touched with sadness and compassion. Then she softly said: "Just *be*."

For people who have complicated their lives as determinedly as I had, this profoundly simple phrase is far more easily said than done. Nana's words planted the seed, but it took me the better part of my lifetime to fully understand, and to occasionally experience the simple freedom of "just being."

Nana died June 26, 1993. I gave (I'm sure with the help of her spirit) the following eulogy for her memorial service:

Nana means "Light" to me.
We are an immensely troubled species we humans
Creating an immensely troubled society on the magnificent earth.
The darkness of our ignorance sometimes seems overwhelming to me,
and probably to many of you.
But Nana could see the indwelling Spirit, the spark of Divinity,
the Light within each of us—within everyone she touched.

Nana was our friend and teacher.
Love and forgiveness were her themes.
Not the needy, possessive emotion we sometimes call love;
But the love with no strings, no conditions,
that is utterly free, whole, and healing,
the Love that is the very essence of the Great Spirit she called
*   Grandfather.*

Grandfather was Nana's friend.
As she spoke to the sea and to the sky and to the sun,
and they answered her,

so she spoke to Grandfather
and was answered.

She taught us that Grandfather dwells in the inner sanctuary of our
hearts,
that we can approach this inner Spirit through forgiveness and Love.
She called this holy place within us the Silence.

It is from this holy place that Nana was born.
It is this loving Silence beyond thought that she served
with all her being, all her life.
And it is this Silence of Perfect Love to which she has returned.

We will miss her. And weep for our loss.
And yet, if we enter the innermost regions of our hearts
through forgiveness and love,
there she will be: arms outstretched, laughing that irresistible laugh,
her eyes bright with the joy of our presence,
her heart bursting with love.

I think Nana was living proof that it *is* possible to live with an open heart, even when times are rough. If I'd ever asked her about this, I imagine she would say, "What's the use of separating yourself from love, ever?"

And yet most of us *do* separate ourselves from love a good deal of the time—I know I do, and the process of abandoning my heart fascinates me.

I've noticed that when I'm judgmental, fearful, frustrated, depressed, angry, and so on, my heart feels closed. Yet when I give my full attention to any of these closed states, my heart opens and there is some degree of radiance again.

For instance, when I'm driving, or sitting in a public place like an airport watching people pass by, I sometimes find myself being absurdly judgmental—how sloppy, how ordinary, how noisy and thoughtless, and so on. At such moments I find my heart completely shut down. Then I remind myself that each of these people is an aspect of God. I drop my expectations and judgments and just see. And my heart opens, and I find myself acknowledging that this is a very hard place we've been born into and the least I can do is wish everyone well—just as they are—just as I am.

How do we know when our inner source of love is open or closed? Expressions like "openhearted" and "put your heart into it" and "have a heart" show our age-old association of the heart area of our bodies with deep feeling, honesty, and love. Ancient wisdom locates the energy of love in the center of the chest behind the sternum.

There may be ways of sensing the opening and closing of the "heart" that have little to do with physical sensation, but I've discovered that it is possible and very useful to actually *feel* the energy of love awaken in my heart. For me it feels like a warm, spacious aliveness, a gentle tingle, a sensation of subtle radiance and well-being.

To discover these feelings it might be helpful to do the following experiment. Find a quiet place and a comfortable chair. Sit with relaxed, alert posture, close your eyes, and put one or both of your hands on the center of your chest. Breathe easily and give your heart area your entire attention.

When we think, we "feel" the thought process just behind our eyes in the center of our heads. When we love, there is a sensation of loving in our hearts. Your hand is placed on the very essence of your self, the home of your soul, the source of love. This indwelling divine vitality is your best and closest friend in the universe. It loves without conditions or judgment of any kind. It sees you exactly as you are, and it loves what it sees, no matter what. This center of love is yours, without interruptions, forever. It is present within you whether you're aware of it or not. Your conscious awareness, however, opens love's radiance to flow through you, transforming you and your world.

Personally I continue to be fascinated by my on-again, off-again relationship with love. I much prefer the on-again times and watch carefully to see what turns me off, or rather what circumstances I use to turn myself off and why. I wonder, can we learn to be as constant a friend of love as love is to us?

WHAT IS:
THE DIVINITY OF NOW

I no longer think of God as a separate deity, but rather as the essential nature of all that is. God is all there is, there is nothing but God, and God is good. By good I don't mean cozy niceness, but that the dynamic nature of spirit tends toward the wholeness of love and (despite appearances) away from harm.

Along with my thesis that there is nothing but the divine, it seems to me that there is nothing but the present moment. The past is gone and the future doesn't yet exist. Obviously, the past leaves its effects on the present, but the past itself is gone. Just as obviously, the present moment affects the next moment, but the future never exists beyond the now, except in our imaginations.

Martin and I love houses. A wise friend and teacher of ours says we have house karma. Over the years we've created several wonderful homes, always remodeling existing structures. Our lifelong goal has been to design and build our dream house. We love living in Hawaii, and for nearly twenty years we've had our eyes on a particularly beautiful house site. About three years ago the lot became available, and to our surprise and delight the owner accepted our first offer. This all happened so easily that we assumed our project was blessed.

This home was to be our final stop and guarantee our future happiness. We hired an architect and created a serene and handsome design that took maximum advantage of the gorgeous setting. We even engaged a top-notch interior designer from the mainland and started thinking about furniture. We were on our way to a nirvana of sand, surf, and sunsets.

We sold our big house in Honolulu, put a lot of stuff in storage, and crammed ourselves and the rest of our possessions into our small beach house in the country to wait for building permits and for construction to begin.

Then, out of the blue, a series of bureaucratic hassles big and small began an endless series of delays and costly legal confrontations. I've lost track of how many times we all said with relief, "Well, that's finally over, now we can begin!" only to be surprised and dismayed by yet another, sometimes whimsical, change in official policy. Permissions granted, permissions withdrawn. Our guarantee of happiness was turning into the prescription for a mix of smoldering rage and clinical depression.

Though we love the sweetness of the people here, over the years we've found the State of Hawaii bureaucrats to be self-important, arbitrary, and downright unfriendly. Our frustration with this latest lengthy fracas with officialdom led us to think seriously about selling the lot and leaving the islands for good. We both felt worn down, hugely disappointed, and unaccountably victimized.

So where is the Christ, where is the Buddha in this mess of frustrated dreams?

One recent afternoon, feeling thoroughly bummed out by all this, I sat down in the living room of the beach house we've owned for twenty-six years and took a long look at the absurdity of letting the supposed source of our future bliss, our imagined tropical Shangri-la, cause us so much unhappiness and angst. I got very quiet and just looked at our situation as objectively as I could. Gazing out the windows, I noticed the sunny perfection of the day and heard the rhythmic rumble of the waves. The plumeria trees were blooming and scenting the breeze, the doves and mynah birds were gabbing. A lamb stew was simmering in the kitchen. Our much-loved dog was asleep at my feet. There wasn't a hint of turmoil anywhere. If I was stressed out, the cause was nowhere in sight. The cause must be in my own head, in my thinking.

It was suddenly clear: I had attached my well-being to an imagined dream house and its easy manifestation. Ignoring past experience, I'd staked my happiness on cooperative, concerned officials and honest, thrifty, competent contractors (good luck!).

And I wondered why it's so easy for me to forget that my sense of well-being is only now in the present. It cannot be dragged in from the past, which is gone, dead and buried, nor can it be found in the future, which doesn't exist. Well-being is simply being well right now, living with as much integrity, clear awareness, and openheartedness as we can muster, with a willingness to examine whatever barriers we're putting in the way of our innate if sometimes elusive wisdom. When I remember to quiet down and do this, the problems that pollute my thinking and vaporize my *wa* (inner harmony) become interesting challenges rather than subversive attachments—I'm free to "be well" and at the same time to vigorously deal with the difficulties at hand. I had been victimized only by my own thinking. I was painfully disappointed not by the officials who were just doing what they do for inscrutable reasons of their own, but by my unrealistic expectations.

It seems to me that the prime reason the potential magnificence of thought so often degrades and works against us is the fact that our thinking is so powerfully programmed and conditioned by the culture we grow up within. We innocently accept current local values, likes and dislikes, prejudices and fears, without much examination and questioning. If it's good enough for Mom and Dad, and for the minister and my teacher and my pals on the playground, too, it's good enough for me.

To bring some order, we have created various societies and, dare I say it, religions. To keep from being raped and pillaged, we get together and devise rules and mythologies—systems of rewards and punishments to achieve a civilized environment in which laws are obeyed, money has value, and in which there is some degree of personal safety and perhaps even freedom. To be effective, these rules and mythologies must be believed. Belief requires indoctrination, which occurs at all levels of civilized life: family traditions, schooling, political rhetoric, advertising, the arts, and the media.

My first memories of being indoctrinated come from very early childhood, when I learned from my parents that if I were a "good boy" (doing what they wanted me to) I would be loved, and when I was a "bad boy" (doing what *I* wanted to do) I would get icy stares, or worse. In short, love is earned by pleasing—which is, as often as not, manipulation at best, downright dishonesty at worst.

As a kid I loved to dance. Put on some music, and I'd be up imitating all the hoofers I'd seen in films. In her youth, the famed ballet dancer Maria Tallchief lived in a duplex apartment across the alley from our house. Tallchief, a Native American, later became one of George Balanchine's favorite dancers at the New York City Ballet; in fact he married her, as he did, in succession, several other of his favorites.

One day, when some neighborhood pals and I were "alley hunting," I found a worn pair of toe shoes and a tattered tutu in Tallchief's trashcan. Imagine the glacial disapproval I received when I ran home, donned tutu and toe shoes, and delightedly danced Swan Lake all over the house. Dad, completely nonplussed, brandished his most lethal sneer. Mom seemed stricken and delivered a freezing version of that "look that kills." And Bill just turned away in disgust. Their learned beliefs told them that a boy jumping around in a tutu was un-American, unholy, and probably illegal! The message was clear: I was a disgrace to the clan, and was summarily cast out, at least for a time. That ancient game of Reward and Punishment, of giving and withdrawing "love" to maintain control, worked like a charm once more. The offending tutu quickly found its way back into Tallchief's trashcan. The message was carved in granite; I never tried *that* again.

A corollary to the "please and conform" syndrome was instilled in

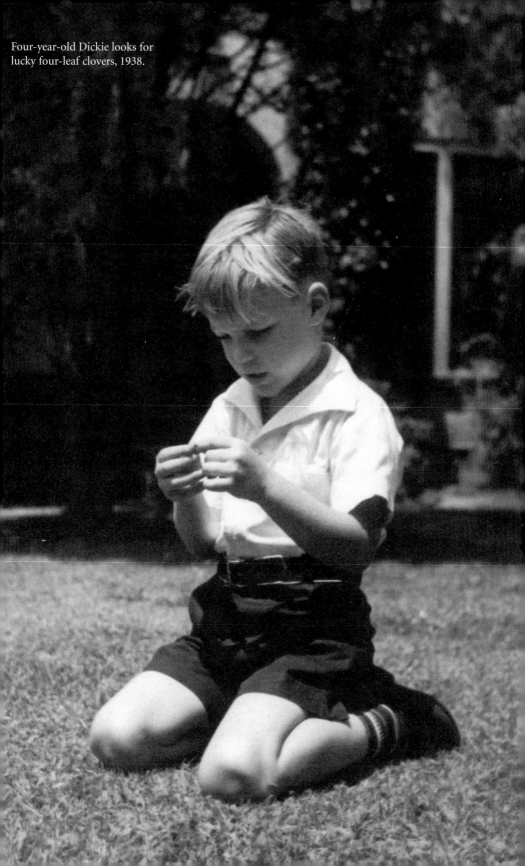

Four-year-old Dickie looks for
lucky four-leaf clovers, 1938.

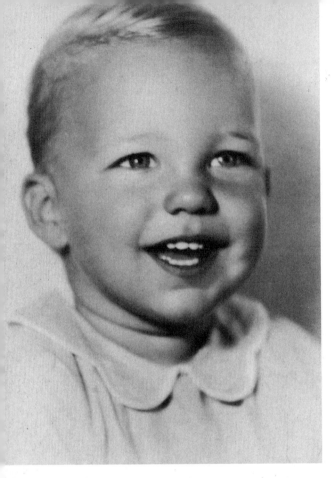

Left: Wee Richard, 1935.

Below: The Chamberlain Magic Show. My shrink took one look at this photo and said, "In that family, you never had a chance." Mother, Elsa; brother, Bill; father, Charles, 1938.

Opposite: A pensive young Richard in a prophetic Hawaiian shirt.

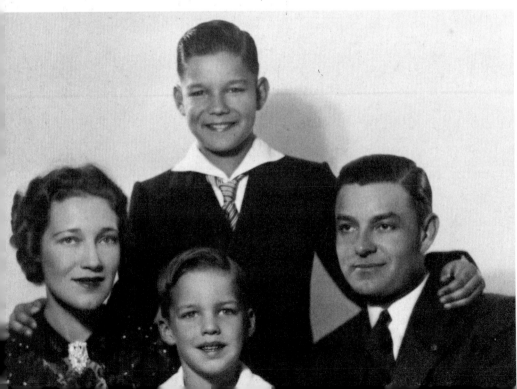

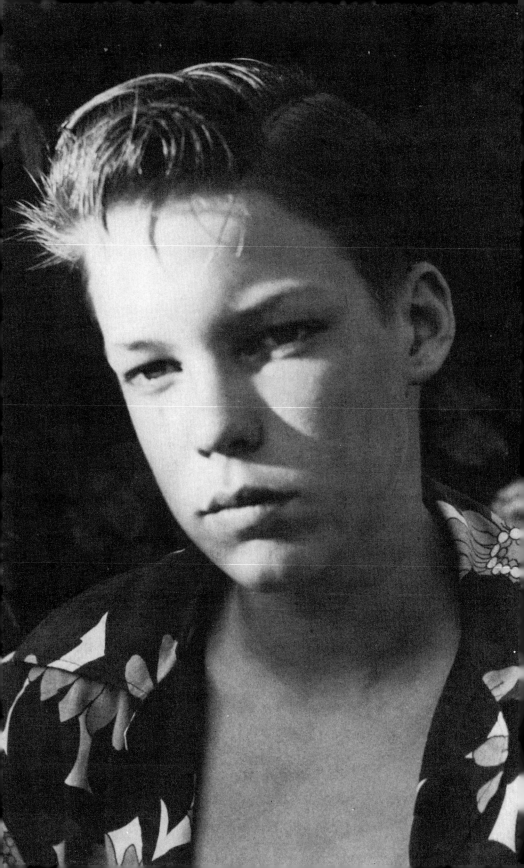

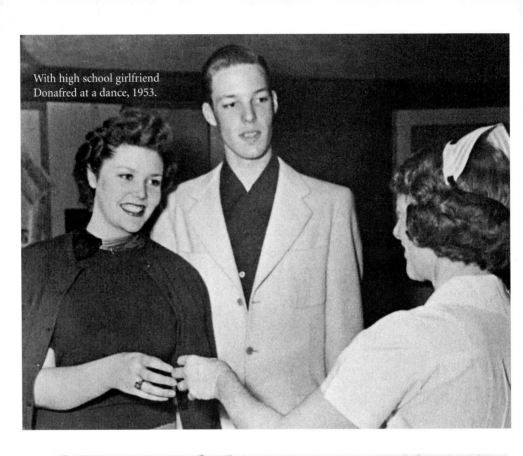

With high school girlfriend Donafred at a dance, 1953.

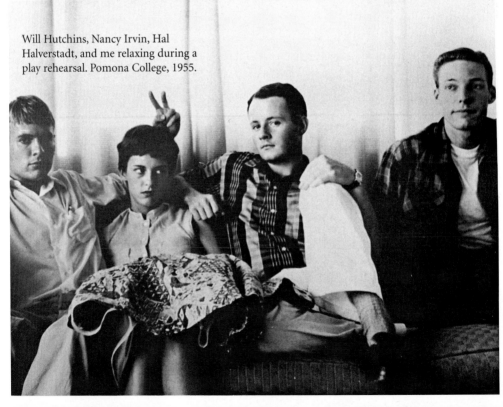

Will Hutchins, Nancy Irvin, Hal Halverstadt, and me relaxing during a play rehearsal. Pomona College, 1955.

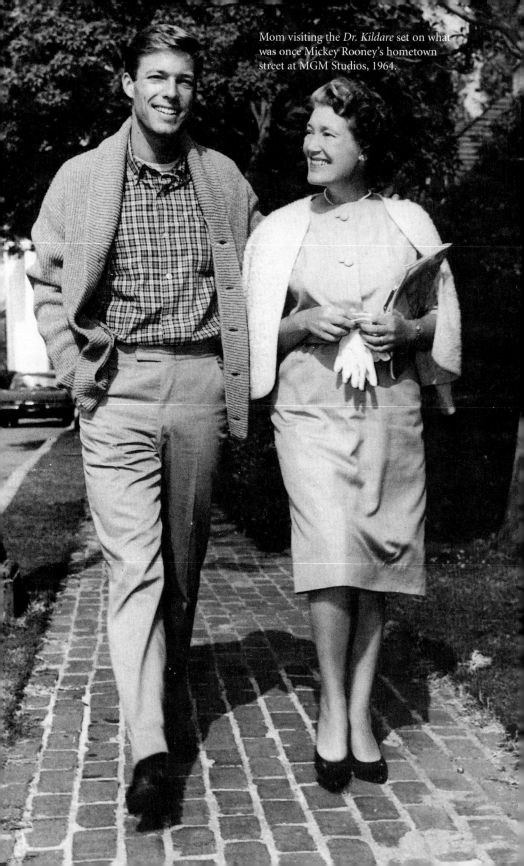

Mom visiting the *Dr. Kildare* set on what was once Mickey Rooney's hometown street at MGM Studios, 1964.

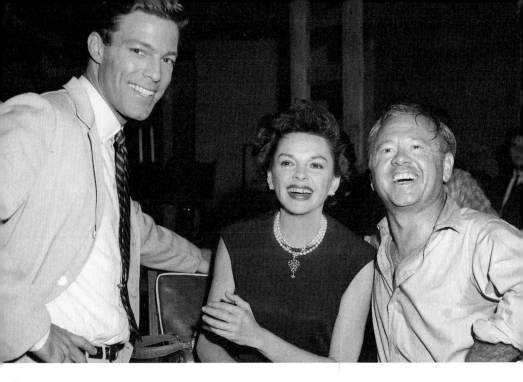

Above: Dr. Kildare meets Judy Garland and Mickey Rooney at MGM Studios. It was wonderful to see how these two former child stars loved each other.

Below: The lab informs Dr. Gillespie that young Kildare's diagnosis was the right one after all. On the set with Raymond Massey, 1964.

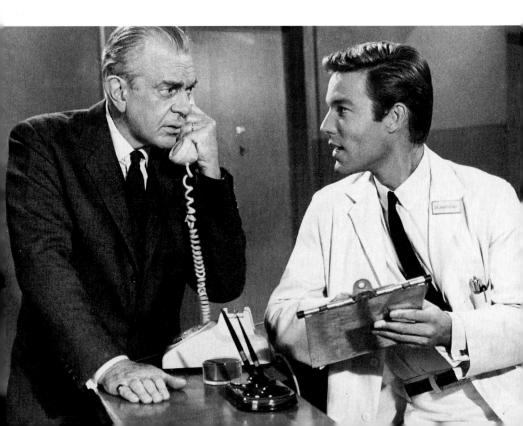

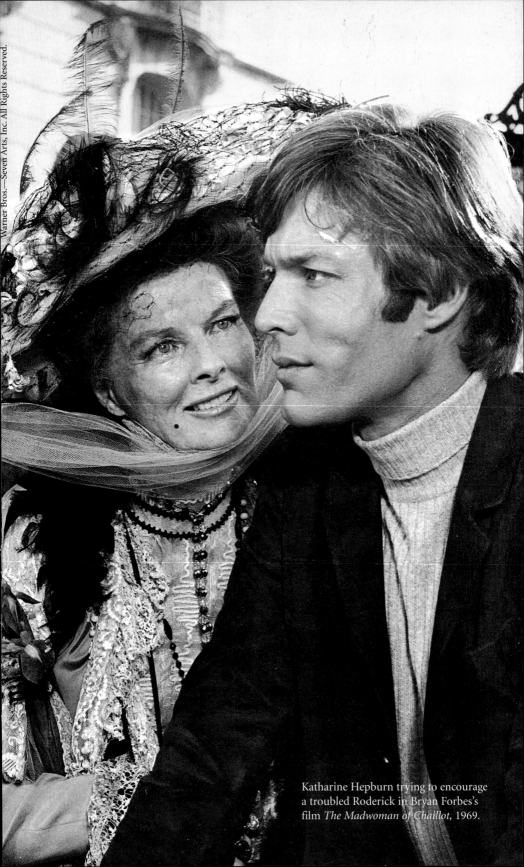

Katharine Hepburn trying to encourage a troubled Roderick in Bryan Forbes's film *The Madwoman of Chaillot*, 1969.

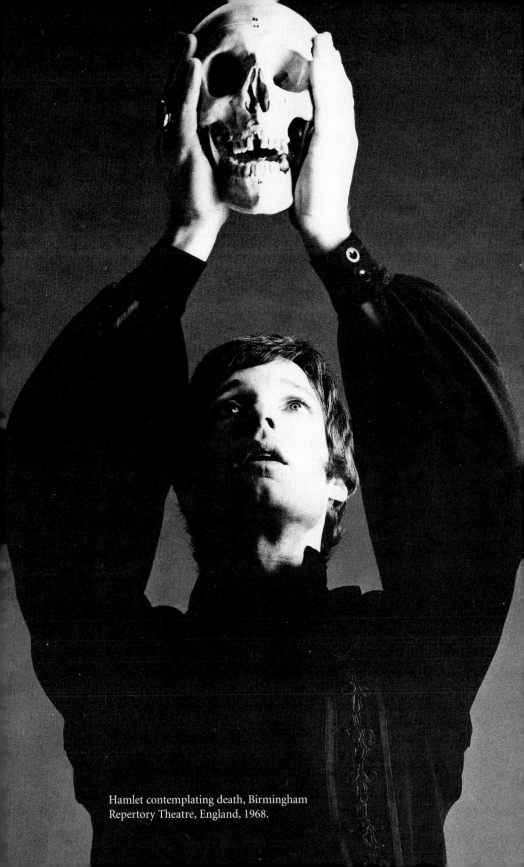

Hamlet contemplating death, Birmingham
Repertory Theatre, England, 1968.

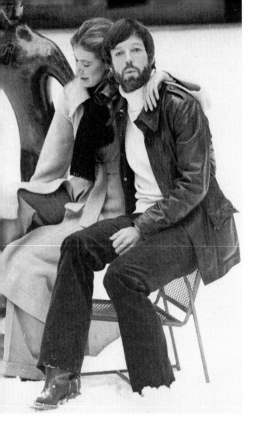

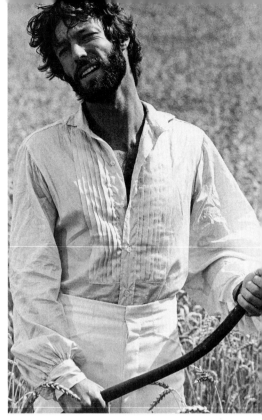

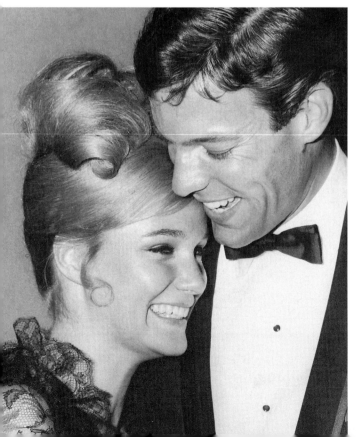

Above left: In the park with fellow actor and dear friend Jennifer Savidge between shows of *The Night of the Iguana* at New York City's Circle in the Square Theatre, 1976.

Above right: Tchaikovsky dreams of a simple life in Ken Russell's *The Music Lovers*, 1970.

Left: With Yvette Mimieux after filming *Joy in the Morning* for MGM, 1965.

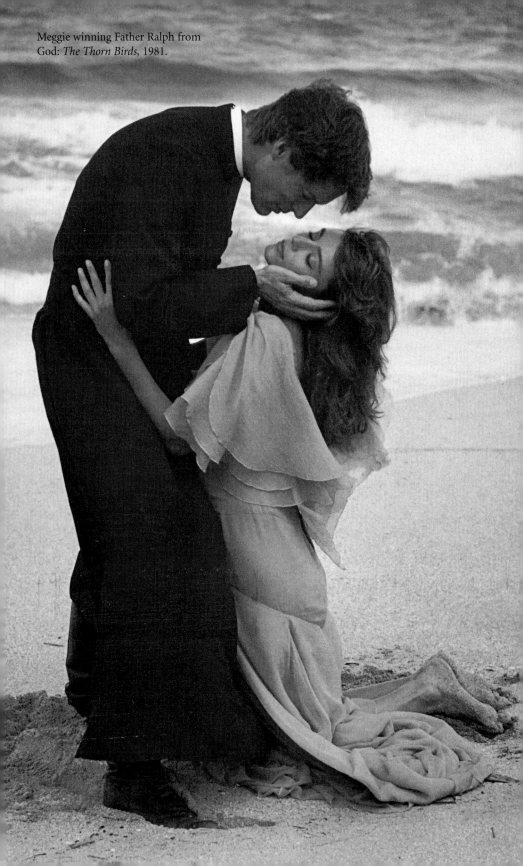

Meggie winning Father Ralph from
God: *The Thorn Birds*, 1981.

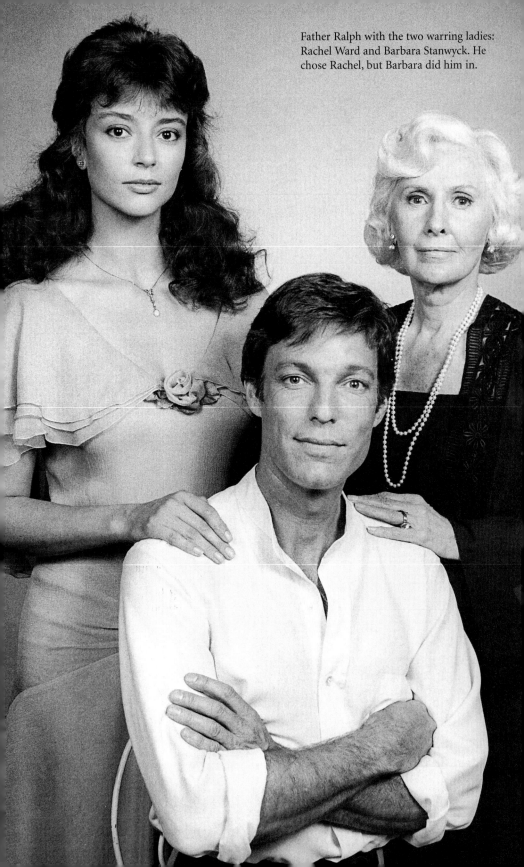

Father Ralph with the two warring ladies: Rachel Ward and Barbara Stanwyck. He chose Rachel, but Barbara did him in.

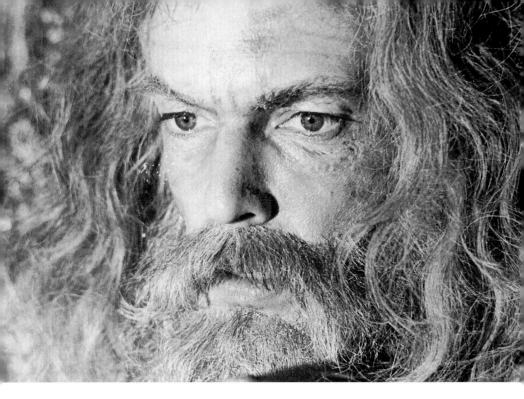

Above: Edmond Dantes wrongfully imprisoned in Norman Rosemont's television production of *The Count of Monte Cristo*, 1975.

Below: Sir Laurence Olivier tells Lord Byron a thing or two on the set of Robert Bolt's film *Lady Caroline Lamb*, 1972.

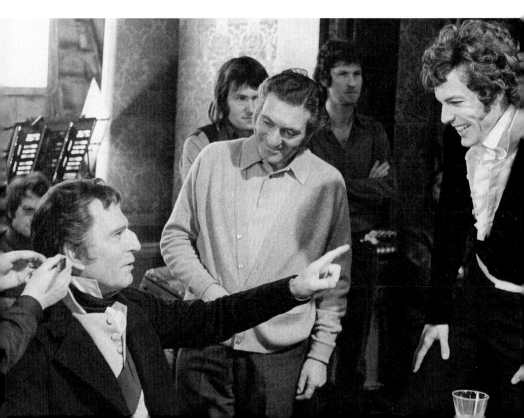

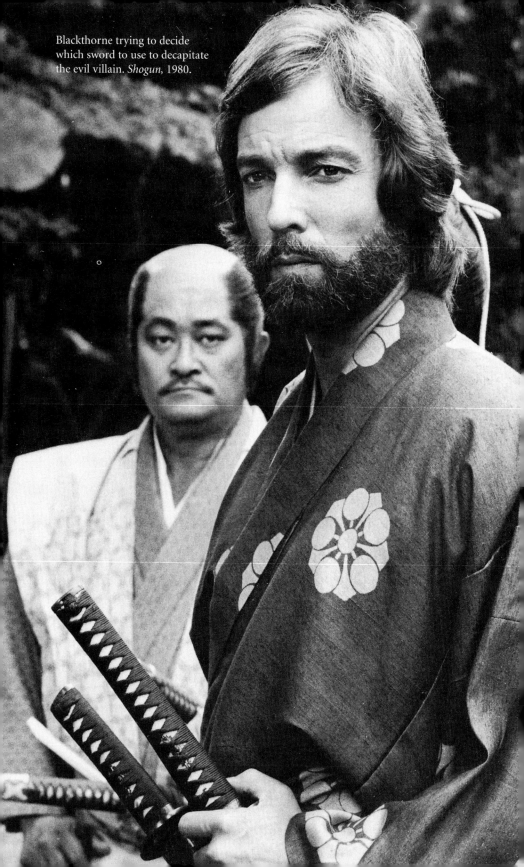

Blackthorne trying to decide which sword to use to decapitate the evil villain. *Shogun*, 1980.

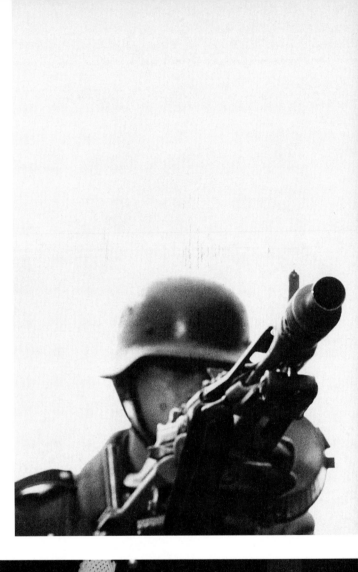

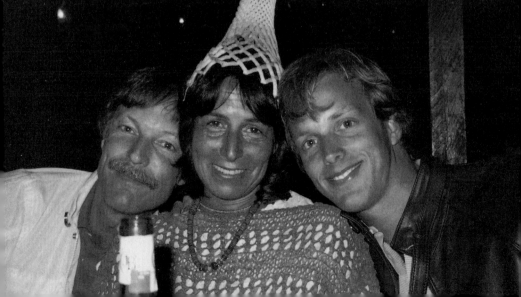

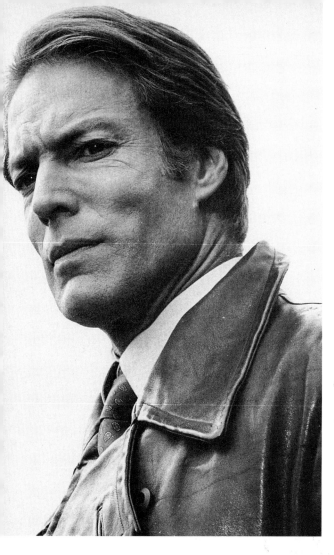

Left: Raoul Wallenberg in big trouble in the television miniseries *Wallenberg: A Hero's Story*, 1985.

Below opposite: With Martin and our good friend Beverly, 1986. The wine seems to have gone to her head.

Below: Good friends Don (my former shrink) and his wife, Roberta, with me and Martin by our hotel's rooftop lotus pond in Ubud, Bali, 2001.

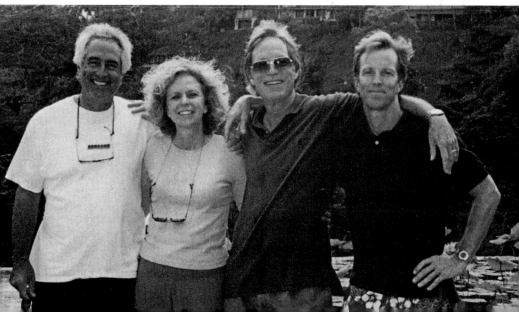

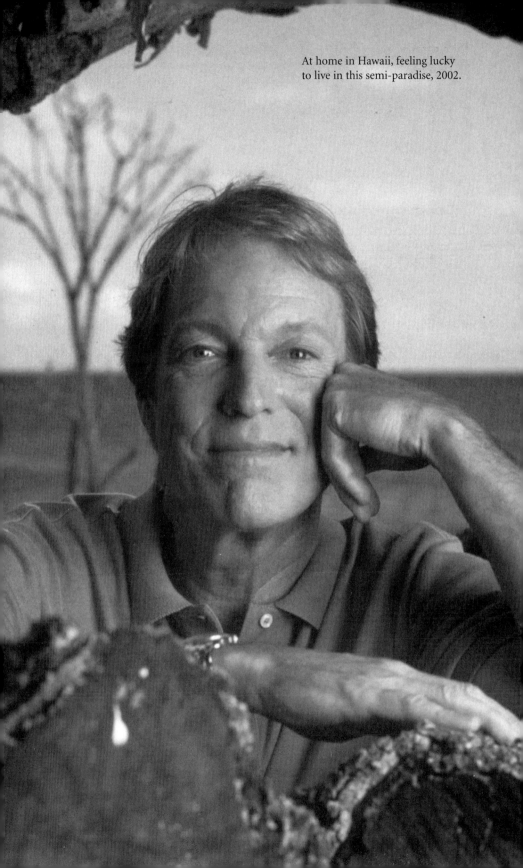

At home in Hawaii, feeling lucky
to live in this semi-paradise, 2002.

my early schooling: *Without my peers' approval I might as well be dead.* We've all experienced the absolute tyranny of the current "ins" and "outs" of any clique of schoolchildren. Before jeans were de rigueur among the grammar school crowd, cords were the thing to wear. Then all at once cords were out, and Levis were mandatory. Cords were more comfortable; I kept wearing them until peer power laughed me off the playground. The tides of conformity are swift and compelling. The fear of being shunned is intense. I switched.

The one area in which I held firm, though it cost me dearly, was team sports, which I loathed and never joined (I think now to my detriment). I enjoyed, and was good at, most other childhood games, but the team gene was left out of my nature.

In the early grades of school I learned that boys must be all boy (rough-and-tumble, combative), girls must be all girl (frilly, domestic, artistic, compassionate, and hopefully not too bright), and any whiff of the androgynous is *verboten*. I was taught early that winning and being *right* are necessary in all circumstances; losing is, like peer disapproval, a kind of death. I learned that I must depend on others for love, approval, and validation in order to merit any degree of worth and happiness (a belief that, if you think about it, is a kind of slavery).

Insofar as a society's tenets create conformity and order in a largely chaotic world, they are obviously useful and necessary. But I can now see that just as obviously these beliefs and mythologies so deeply imprinted on my brain eventually inhibit my longing for psychological and spiritual truth, for self-discovery. In the long run, conformity doesn't elevate me to wisdom, it puts me to sleep.

Every day I encounter evidence of my preprogrammed thought patterns and beliefs that remain unexamined and therefore continue to obstruct my openhearted love of life. All the indoctrinations of my youth still linger in the corners of my mind. My job now is to embrace these learned and often arbitrary thought patterns, fears, and prejudices, with awareness and inquiry, to dissolve them in the light of love and understanding. The examined life is the *only* life worth living, and the reality of what *is* is the only place worth living in.

When I was about four years old, the photographer son of my grandmother's great and classy friend Lee Maynard organized a photo session in the front yard of Lee's home in Los Angeles to photograph Nonnie and then me. I remember that day well. Lee's son saw that I was shy so he asked me to look for four-leaf clovers in the lawn to make me less self-conscious. I searched and the camera clicked.

Just the other day, while packing up to move into our new house, I came across the resulting sunny photo of myself as a rather lost little blond boy in short pants looking for cloverleafs in the grass. As I gazed at this distant image, I immediately felt I could love this kid with all my heart. How I would love to take him in my arms and spend time with him, getting to know who he was, whatever his problems and quirks.

His actual parents, of course, had tried to dictate who he was. They wanted him to conform to their image of a "proper" son, and they were annoyed and anxious when he resisted being turned into their poster boy.

Looking at this photo, taken over sixty years ago, my instincts were totally opposite. I'd be charmed by Dick's dancing. I'd be fascinated to find out why he stubbornly refused to learn to tie his shoes or write his name, why he feared school and had such a dislike for reading. I'd encourage his daydreams and his love of art and music. I'd lead him into learning through an appreciation of *his* interests rather than my own. I would love him and honor him just as he was.

Thus, by respecting what is, I would not have burdened this kid with fear and self-loathing, trying to shame him into being what *I wanted* him to be. With careful guidance I'd let him prosper as himself. And somehow I'd try to teach him that all the necessary shoulds and musts that accompany growing up would eventually, if fully understood, lead not to the dull constrictions of conformity, but could eventually be discarded in favor of the vitality of freedom and genuine self-discovery.

Sidestepping our learned ideals of what *should* be and giving the reality of what *is* at this moment our entire attention, our whole, open-hearted awareness (being aware of our expectations and "shoulds" as well) is I think not only the prerequisite for wise change but also the opening to Christ, to Buddha, to the sacred. If the divine isn't present in what's happening within, to, and around us right now, it isn't anywhere. I think what is, right now, is governed by the laws of God's nature, in fact it *is* God. In this sense the traits we would prefer to disown (like our greed, our anxiety, and our arrogance) become not enemies, but our friends, signaling to us that our thinking is off base.

What *is* at each moment, no matter how magnificent, boring, or devastating, is where divinity lives. I think every atom of existence is sacred. We'd like to pick and choose our moments, finding God in some and the devil in others. But each moment, without exception, is a manifestation of the divine. We simply haven't expanded our awareness enough to feel the sacred everywhere.

If my sense of the ubiquitous nature of divinity is a fact, then each moment of life's ups and downs, joys and sorrows—whether or not it is what we *want*, whether or not we judge it good or bad—is an opportunity for communion with the sacred. This detached, undistorted seeing opens our being to the natural flowering of our hearts, our spirit, our wisdom, and to acting rightly in the present situation. For at the center of each of us is the sacredness, the love we so desperately seek elsewhere. And that, I suspect, is life's favorite irony.

All of these beliefs ring true to me, but what do they really mean? How can we love reality, *what is,* when reality is so often *not* what we expect or want?

The other day I was about half an hour into a long drive to the Honolulu airport when I discovered that I'd left my wallet, with driver's license, cash, and credit cards, in my bedroom drawer. I had no choice: I had to drive back home, waste an hour of valuable time, and miss my plane. I was furious with myself, frustrated by my carelessness, hating the whole stupid process of finding the right freeway exit and circling back for my stupid wallet. I worried that I might not be able to get a later flight.

As I drove home, I was flailing myself with stories of disaster and my flagrant ineptitude, when suddenly I thought, "Wait a minute—what's really happening here?"

The truth of the situation was starkly simple: I was a person driving a very nice car to a beautiful house to pick up a wallet and phone for a later reservation. It wasn't the first time I've forgotten my wallet, and it probably won't be the last. With this clear, unadorned view of what was happening, my self-flagellating inner Greek tragedy lost all its drama and became comic. I was free to drop it, enjoy the gorgeous island scenery, and listen to my favorite program on NPR. In short, I stopped fighting reality and got happy smack in the middle of what is right now.

BENEDICT CANYON

With some regret, in 1980 we left our New York City apartment, our first home, and bought a small ranch house in Benedict Canyon, a somewhat rustic retreat in the hills above Los Angeles. There were still hints of the wild—deer and coyotes roamed the underbrush and California oak trees.

After extensive remodeling the house took on a slightly Japanese proportion and serenity. I had purchased several beautiful screens and scrolls from the various *Shogun* sets, and Martin and I had found a number of striking pieces in Kyoto on a previous trip to Japan. My favorite feature of the house was a large spa bathtub with a broad shoji screen that opened onto a lovely Asian rock garden and hillside.

The main treasure we found in Kyoto was a large four-paneled screen of poetic calligraphy by the great Shoyo Morita. We designed the living room around this beautifully simple piece, presenting it in a long tokonoma that dominated the room. In Japan, a tokonoma is a special space dedicated to a work of art such as a screen or scroll, and perhaps a flower arrangement.

When the first heavy rainstorm hit our newly remodeled house, the roof sprang one small but lethal leak that during the night tragically aimed its single stream of water directly on the Morita. The soggy rice paper screen was a heartbreaking sight the next morning. We sent this prize possession to various art restoration experts, but no one could put Humpty together again.

On the brighter side, Martin had given me a dalmatian puppy for my birthday weeks before we moved in. We named this frisky little guy Billy Boy, but instead of bonding with me, Billy fell for Martin in a big way. They'd even sing together. Feeling a bit left out, I went to Billy Boy's breeder and bought his half sister, Jesse.

Jesse was a beauty, aristocratic in bearing, intelligent, blatantly neurotic, and an accomplished actress. She could, for instance, pretend to be in terrible pain just to get attention. During these feigned episodes we'd take her to the vet just in case, but invariably she turned out to be fit as a fiddle.

Following one of her dramatic performances I decided to examine *my* side of our relationship and realized that, like some thoughtless parents, I loved Jesse when she behaved well and didn't when she didn't. Upon her return from the vet I sat down with her in our front garden and told her that from then on I loved her all the time, no matter what, and I meant it. She never feigned illness again.

Jesse was unique—I've never met another dog like her. Despite the complexity of our relationship, or perhaps because of it, I was very attached to this four-legged, brown-spotted creature who seemed at times to have the soul of a disappointed lover from a past life, revisiting me in a form that, alas, would assure her continued disappointment.

Jesse's eccentricities only added interest to her charmed life as one of two beloved household pets until advancing age began its inevitable subtractions.

Near the end of Jesse's fourteenth year she was suffering so badly from arthritis that she couldn't even lie down in her bed without yelping with pain. After consulting her vet, I decided very reluctantly to have her put down. Jesse still loved people food, so on the fateful morning I cooked her scrambled eggs and buttered toast for breakfast. She loved the treat. Then our vet came to the house and while I held Jesse on my lap (she knew what was coming, but barely resisted) the vet gave her a shot in her front leg and slowly Jesse went to sleep and then died.

I had never witnessed a death before and it was heartbreaking. The second her body ceased functioning this unique being vanished from the world. Her limp carcass, still warm, was there in my arms, but Jesse was irretrievably gone.

It seemed so clear at that moment that Jesse's body, though instrumental in expressing her spirit, was not itself her spirit, her life force, her personality. Her spirit inhabited her body but was something other than body, beyond the physical. Our bodies seem unquestionably individual and separate, but is each *life* individual and separate? Could it be that we all share one life just as we all share one air, one water, one sun? Could it be that humanity is actually a unified being of which each of us is a single, essential cell? Could there be one mind thinking our thoughts and one soul overlighting our being? These questions and their implications interest me a lot. Perhaps, though unique, we are not separate at all. Blood is blood, thought is thought, breath is breath, suffering is suffering, joy is joy, love is love.

Imagine a room full of candles of different colors, sizes, shapes, and scents. A candle's purpose is to give light. A candle, whatever its shape, is brought to life by fire. Now imagine lighting each of these candles with one match. The candles are now enlivened by separate flames of the same fire. And the glow that each candle emits blends with all the other lights into one roomful of indivisible light.

The brother/sisterhood of humanity seems so good, so noble as an ideal, but feels like a hair shirt when we actually try it on. Imagine facing Osama bin Laden and embracing him as your brother, as in fact a version of yourself. I can barely imagine realizing that the madness of his zealots is a version of my own zealotry. Where do I put my hatred?

As we resist comparing ourselves to this or any "satanic" creature, let's take a long look inside. Consider how fanatically we cling to our self-image and images we construct of our husbands and wives and children. Consider how fanatically we cling to our conditioned thinking—all the stuff we're force-fed by our particular families, cultures, and political spin wizards. Consider how ruthlessly we hold on to the stories we tell ourselves about our own superiority or inferiority and about our versions of God. Consider how fanatically most of us avoid any clear-sighted observation of our destructive patterns of thought and all the negative stuff we carelessly put up with in ourselves. Nearly all of us are to some degree fanatics.

I tend to hate and fear in others exactly what I fear and disown in myself. In this sense the people who irritate me the most are often superbly accurate mirrors reflecting back to me aspects of myself that I try to hide, like neediness, pushiness, selfishness, and degrees of violence. And for this invaluable service the people I dislike deserve my thanks. There is a Buddhist saying: "Be grateful to everyone." Exceedingly good advice if you think about it.

DREAMING ON HIGH

Martin and I missed a lot of things about living on the East Coast—all the excitement and the cultural richness of New York City. But we found that Los Angeles offered its own brand of riches. We gathered a wonderful group of new friends—a motley crew of therapists, acupuncturists, a few show biz types, and a spiritual teacher or two. And we were interested in the various explorations of consciousness going on—some serious, some not—in the early eighties. We tried out a number of "California" activities like getting "rolfed" and floating in isolation tanks. We even got involved briefly with a pretty blond housewife who "channeled" an ancient and exotically alluring spiritual potentate of some kind. All this was new to us, and we cast our lines in many directions with varying luck.

One big nourishing fish we caught was a meditation group that met several times a year. The group consisted mainly of Gestalt therapists. The group originally wanted to discover or enhance our intuitive and psychic abilities and was led by a woman known for her gifts in this field. The group eventually met without the leader and developed into a loving extended family who encouraged one another's inner development as evidenced in our outer lives.

Another arena of the New Age California experience that was quite spectacular occurred accidentally. In China, while walking on the Great Wall, Martin connected with an intriguing older woman from Marin who told him that she led blindfolded LSD trips as a means of accelerating one's spiritual awareness.

When he told me about this, I said, "Blindfolded?" I thought the purpose of LSD was to "see" the world from a different viewpoint. Well, Martin, ever fearful of the loss of control that drug-induced states offer, was intrigued for the first time in his life. So was I. The idea of accelerating enlightenment was naïve, and yet tempting. Eventually, we both ended up in the temple of the "Priestess," where we ingested the "omniscient" LSD with our blindfolds in place. The experience lasted through the night as she played on multiple music players various symphonies, recorded poems, and speeches, such as the one John Glenn made when he first orbited earth.

As the LSD took effect and the music soared, we sailed off into our own orbits. I drifted into a state of transcendental beauty that was beyond imagination and lasted through the night.

The most illuminating moments of this experience gave me the sense of the vaster dimensions of our beings. I felt that my self was like a handful of brightly colored beads organized together in love, not by my mind's image of myself. Again and again I joyously cast these particles of my being out among the myriad particles of the music, knowing that if life wished me to reunite as Richard, I would. If not, my particles would mix with equal lovingness with the rest of creation. There simply is nothing to lose.

We knew that drugs could be dangerous and that we were taking a risk. And it would be easy to dismiss the resulting experience as illusory and lacking significance. But my extraordinary vision has stayed with me all these years. I feel as if I had been briefly admitted into a level of esoteric truth that is genuine.

THE THORN BIRDS

This exploration of consciousness California style was interrupted by a great tsunami of the miniseries, roaring with incredible speed and aquatic power through the shoals of *Shogun* and crashing with equal might onto the steamy shores of Australia.

When I read *The Thorn Birds,* Colleen McCullough's epic novel about the travails of an Australian family, I immediately knew this passionate love story cried out to be a great television miniseries. I also knew that I *had* to play Father Ralph, a character whose stature and complexity seemed to me an irresistible challenge.

The suspenseful scenario of being cast as Father Ralph was an almost exact repeat of the casting of John Blackthorne except that the enormous success of *Shogun* gave me a lot more clout.

One of the major studios first attempted to transform *The Thorn Birds* into a feature film directed by Peter Weir, again starring Robert Redford as the troubled priest. Like *Shogun,* the novel proved far too long and complicated to be distilled into a two- or three-hour film, and the property was sold to ABC television. Only the miniseries format could be expanded to contain the entire story. Again I waited in line and was finally tapped for the immensely gifted, but ultimately doomed character of Ralph de Bricassart.

Casting Meggie took a bit longer, as many actresses were clamoring for this plum role. Only Jane Seymour and Rachel Ward made the final round. We filmed two screen tests, and both Jane and Rachel were excellent. Jane was more experienced and assured, but I suspect Rachel won the part because she *wasn't* so assured and therefore seemed more vulnerable. I, on the other hand, was terrible in both tests and was surprised when the network didn't fire me on the spot. I hadn't yet figured out how to play Ralph so I waffled around lacking conviction. I also made the fatal mistake of dying my hair black for the test, thinking this would give me a certain dark Irish glamour. Instead I ended up looking like a performing seal with a hangover. I must have had an ironclad contract, because ABC kept me on.

With Meggie cast and shooting almost ready to begin, I read the novel over and over again preparing for the job of actually becoming Father Ralph. I found him quite elusive until I realized that my predicament in life was somewhat similar to his. Ralph's heart was torn into thirds, mine into halves.

Our young priest was exceedingly ambitious and loved the glamour and hierarchical power of the Catholic Church. He had a genuine vocation to serve Spirit and vowed his life to Christ. He also loved Meggie with all the passion and deep caring that a man feels for his soul mate. Even when she was a child, Ralph recognized in Meggie his other half, the woman he was destined to love. Ralph's tragic dilemma was the incompatibility of his three loves: the glamour of power, his vows to the Christ, and his love of the one thing the Church most feared—a woman. Though Ralph had considerable success in all three of these conflicting loves—he advanced to the high rank of cardinal, he served humanity by covertly opposing the Nazis, and he won Meggie's heart— he could fully commit to none and was ultimately torn apart and died lost and defeated.

Though my own inner conflicts hadn't risen (or descended) to tragedy, I too felt torn and painfully bifurcated. It was as if I were two people who were bound together but unable to be friends. I was dedicated to building my glamorous career and the public image I thought the world demanded, and I regarded aspects of my quite different private self with disapproval and fear. For Ralph the force of rigid Church doctrine was the culprit, for me the bogeymen were the mores and expectations of my public and my own self-rejection.

So I began to feel akin to Father Ralph, my brother in confusion, and I liked and felt compassion for him from the start. How sad that he was the one thorn bird who, having impaled himself on the sword of his own brilliance, never found his song.

Playing Ralph's love for Meggie was a cinch. Rachel Ward was uniquely beautiful, passionate, and blissfully in love. In reality Rachel hadn't fallen in love with either me or Ralph—early in the shoot she fell head over heels for Bryan Brown, the handsome Australian actor who played Luke, Meggie's no-good and perennially absent husband whom she had married to spite the perennially absent Ralph. But as Father Ralph it was easy to believe the radiance of her love was for me and me alone.

The Thorn Birds producer Stan Margulies and our screenwriter Carmen Culver did a masterful job of streamlining McCullough's novel for its televised incarnation, but we had major disagreements about Father Ralph's character. As I've said, I saw Ralph as torn apart by conflicting, but genuine loves, whereas they saw him as rather a cad, driven solely by lust and ambition. (Secretly I too felt there was a dash of cad in him, but that was far from his whole story.)

We had fiery meetings and I wrote endless letters concerning several of Ralph's scenes where I thought he seemed too duplicitous, but they were reluctant to change a word of the script. So speaking *their* words I did the best I could to keep Ralph's character on *my* track. Obviously Ralph was extremely ambitious, but that was just one aspect of his dilemma. I felt he'd be much more interesting and compelling if his incompatible loves for God and for Meggie were both painfully real.

Despite our literary differences Carmen Culver and I found each other very funny and through our laughter we became good friends. During the last few weeks of shooting the Queensland sugar cane scenes

on the Hawaiian island of Kauai, I took Carmen to that rarest of eater-
ies: a really good Mexican restaurant. Over several margaritas I tried for
the last time to make clear my ideas about Father Ralph. "Oh," she
exclaimed, "so *that's* what you meant. Well, of course I think you were
right." I was struck dumb. After a long pause we both started laughing—me through my tears.

Barbara Stanwyck's professionalism was legendary in Hollywood.
Along with her astonishing youthfulness at seventy-something, she was
known as one of the master craftsmen of film acting. At our first read-
through (she was playing the willful Mary Carson) she not only knew
all her lines, but every flick of her eyes. Several times she said to our
cameraman who was present at the reading, "You *will* be sure to catch
that look, won't you." I've never seen an actor that well prepared so early
in the game.

Film acting involves shooting the same scene many times from different angles for editing and to get just the right performances. Most
actors slightly vary their performance from take to take to keep things
alive. But no matter how many times we'd shoot our scenes together,
Stanwyck always played every moment exactly the same, even in the
beginning rehearsals. And yet her performance was always fresh, new,
and strongly related to those of the other actors. I don't know how she
did it, but that was her technique, her method, and it worked like gangbusters.

She was unflappable. Excepting one scene in which she encounters
Father Ralph on the veranda of Drogheda during a tremendous down-
pour. Ralph, thinking himself alone, has just stripped off all his wet
clothes when Mary (Stanwyck) appears and comes on to him. For the
one and only time on the whole production Stanwyck flubbed her lines,
which surprised her as much as the rest of us. After a stunned pause she
murmured, "Well, it's been a *very* long time since I've stood next to a
naked man."

She'd usually arrive at work around five A.M., long before the rest of us, and sit around drinking coffee and shooting the bull with the crew. Our cameraman used a lot of atmospheric smoke—really horrible stuff, hard on the throat, hard on the lungs—in the interior sets. Except when we were shooting I'd stay as far away as possible from this artificial smog, but Stanwyck would just sit there in the haze and schmooze while they were lighting. This was, I fear, a big mistake because she'd had pneumonia six months earlier, and I suspect breathing all that phony smoke actually hastened her death.

Daryl Duke, a craggy, white-bearded Canadian was our superb director. Daryl had more faith in our story and cast than either the network or our producers, and he created a lavish production that none of them were happy to pay for. We actors adored him, but he got himself into deep trouble with the powers that were. Even after the smashing success of *The Thorn Birds* all over the world, even after the huge profits began to roll in, they resisted giving Daryl credit. I remember when we received various awards for the show, the producers wouldn't even mention Daryl's name. By default it was left to me to thank him for his invaluable contribution to our success.

If revving up your infatuated couple to intolerable heights of desire and then jamming insurmountable obstacles between them makes a great love story, then *The Thorn Birds* is one of the all-time great sagas of passion. Meggie, the irresistible, meeting Ralph, the unattainable. What woman wouldn't lust after the beautiful, remote young man who's given his life to God? What young man of God couldn't help but long for the forbidden warmth of gorgeous Meggie? This is a love story made in heaven to put its lovers through hell. And yet in their stolen moments together, Ralph and Meggie loved totally, recklessly, absolutely. How many of us can claim to have dared the same?

The parable that figures so importantly in this story tells us of a particular kind of bird that throughout its life is unable to sing until at the end it encounters a thorn tree. The bird then impales itself on one of the thorns and in its mortal pain it sings a song so beautiful that it stops

God in His tracks. He and all the angels turn to listen. In short, only through our suffering can we discover the extravagant beauties of life.

Obviously there's some validity in this premise, but I've always had trouble trying to figure out why the sacred forces of creation, which I believe are essentially wisdom and love, seem to require so much hardship along our paths toward our wholehearted experience of compassion and truth.

SHATTERED LOVE

Relying on a great deal of evidence, today's astronomers and physicists theorize that a number of billions of years ago, prior to the primal explosion of the "Big Bang" that created our universe, there was nothing: no time, no space, no thing visible or temporal at all. Whatever it was that exploded into all that is was some sort of invisible perfection utterly beyond the understanding of science.

My premise is that this invisible ground of being, this uncaused cause that preceded existence is divinity itself, the stupendous, immaterial power of creative love. Love is perfect unity, perfect wholeness transcending time and space, beyond the particular, utterly indivisible and impersonal. And yet, the divine contains within the mystery of its perfect wholeness a dynamic creativity and stupendous curiosity.

Only such perfection, such faultless eternal power would dare to shatter itself into time and space, into every conceivable potential of its nature, into everything it seemed not to be. God seems to be exploring its own being with total fascination and with no reservations whatsoever.

And that's where we humans become useful. We are a manifestation of divine curiosity. We are shattered love. We splintered human beings embody a divine inquiry into its own eternal nature. God has shattered its perfection just as a prism shatters the wholeness of white light into the infinite variety of its various wavelengths and resulting colors. It is this divine exploration that has created the destiny of the thorn bird and us and our experience of the dark side.

If I am honest with myself, I see that in the right circumstances I would to some degree be capable of absolutely anything any human being has ever done or will ever do—this includes the entire spectrum from Hitler to Saint Francis. Given the right conditions, I might have become a serial killer or the baptizer of Christ. Each of us contains *all* the possibilities of power. From the most sublime to the most grotesque, *all* power in this world is a shard of the original holiness of love.

Each of us is a prism of shattered love. The seven energy centers of our bodies refract divine energy into a surprisingly perfect rainbow of various aspects or qualities of our life force.

Certain ancient philosophies have been aware of these seven major energy centers (called chakras) for centuries. The first center in the groin has to do with survival, commitment to life, the intense desire to exist in this physical world. The character of this survival energy can range from the bucolic harmony of farming to the brutality of war. Its color (for those who can see such things) is red. The second chakra just above the genitals is sexual, procreative, the intoxicating energies of species survival. The often overwhelming intensity of this energy can vary in quality from love to rape. Its color is orange. The third chakra in the solar plexus is the center of emotion and personal power (we know how various *those* can be). Its color is yellow. The fourth chakra is within the heart area, and its quality is love. Neither sexual nor emotional (though it can inform both), this energy when awakened radiates the eternal warmth of divine love and is incorruptible. Its color is green. The fifth chakra at the throat is creativity and expression. Its color is blue. The sixth chakra is in the middle of the forehead and is the center of both intellect and insight, thought and the inner knowing beyond thought. Its color is purple. The seventh or crown chakra is at the top of the head and is our connection with the greater divine. Its color is white.

So each of us is in this sense a stack of divine love shattered into its variously colored component possibilities ranging from the most primitive to the sublime. And we're rescued from chaos by the placement at the very center of ourselves (the heart chakra) of the balancing, unifying energy of love *complete*, right in the midst of love *shattered*.

The temporal world we live in is also shattered divinity. We are individual laboratories of self-discovery inhabiting the universal arena of divine self-exploration and revelation. Our individual self-discovery is essential to the revelation of the divine nature. We are love exploring love. We are love refracted, discovering all the potential aspects, dark and light, of its holy self.

THE NINETIES

The final decade of the twentieth century seemed to me to be in a terrific hurry to get itself over with. Years sped by with reckless nonchalance. The mammoth miniseries like *Centennial, Shogun, Wallenberg, The Bourne Identity, Dream West,* and *The Thorn Birds* that dominated earthly television and my career in the 1980s were rendered extinct by the disastrous (for the three TV networks) collision with that hurtling meteor Cable Television. The proliferation of cable channels divided and scattered our viewing audience and thus starved the networks of the abundant greenbacks needed to feed those spectacular dinosaurs of epic television. Though it would take time for me to realize it, the golden age of my long career would begin to fade along with the eighties. And yet a lot of interesting work continued to come my way.

The 1990s swirled in on the winds of change. Martin and I had been living in Los Angeles and occasionally flying to our Hawaiian beach house for brief holidays. But each time we had to drag ourselves back to L.A. we found it harder to leave our island paradise. So we came up with a plan that shook up our lives big-time.

We created a Hawaii-based television series called *Island Son* about a *haole* (Caucasian) who had been brought up as the *hanai* (adopted) son of a traditional Hawaiian family. His father was a *kahuna* (master) of the ancient healing arts. Throughout his youth his father taught his haole son the medicinal secrets of his ancestors, and as an adult he attained a western medical degree to balance his nontraditional medical background. Our idea was to make the show about the real Hawaii, ancient and modern, and its local people. We wanted to share all we'd learned about the wonderful and mysterious aspects of Hawaiian culture that tourists rarely get a chance to experience—their healing arts and spiritual life, their closeness to nature, and the aloha of the land.

CBS seemed to agree with the plan, but unbeknownst to us they were really planning a sort of *Dr. Kildare Goes Hawaiian,* which wasn't what we had in mind at all.

We moved to Oahu and began shooting *Island Son* with Martin as island-side coexecutive producer. Unfortunately for us, CBS controlled the mainland producers and writers. Despite our protests, the Hawaiian themes got watered down, and we ended up with a standard doctor show with a Hawaiian backdrop. *C'est la vie.* Mercifully, at our insistence, the show ended after the first season. On the plus side, *Island Son* got us to Hawaii full-time.

A new and unsettling period began for me after the demise of our television series.

To begin with, some gay activist cowboy started investigating and publicly "outing" celebrity types. He claimed his vision was to offer up worthy role models to gay youth, but I figured his real motivation was envy, anger, and a misguided hunger for power. In any case, the ever-predictable tabloids flashed front-page headlines that I was gay, shoving me right into the middle of my darkest nightmares.

My fears were threefold. First, I was terrified that this news would alienate fans and topple my cherished career, robbing me of the work I loved and my only source of income. Second, the elaborate and pristine self-image I had created, sustained, and lived suddenly smashed into shambles around my bare feet, sharp edges drawing blood everywhere. And third, I had to begin to acknowledge and deal with my long buried self-loathing and "subjective phobia." From early youth I had absorbed our culture's general fear of any sort of gender confusion, giving my utterly harmless sexual orientation the undeserved semblance of villainy. I had to admit to myself that I was as homophobic as the public I sought to please. When we cling obdurately to our soap operas, life has a way of grabbing us by the scruff and beating the daylights into us.

After almost a decade of personal inner work and work with Martin, the silver lining of these murky clouds has gradually appeared. Very recently it has dawned on me that this whole painful drama of fear and loathing, of guilt and perversity, is a blatant travesty of reality. Sexual orientation is a benign personal matter; it is a total nonissue, of no public importance whatsoever. As I understand it, about ninety-five percent of any society is heterosexual and something like five percent is homosexual. A few heterosexuals are exceptionally fine, creative, and compassionate; the vast majority are hardworking, tax-paying, kind, upstanding citizens; and a few are trouble. A few homosexuals are exceptionally fine, creative, and compassionate; the vast majority are hardworking, tax-paying, kind, upstanding citizens; and a few are trouble. Statistically it's all about the same. Without the blinders of ignorance and prejudice there is no sound reason we should not get along with each other just fine.

I learned to dislike gay people, myself included, from my family, and from my peers, who in their youth were frantic to prove their normalcy by quite viciously rejecting anything "abnormal" in themselves and, by extension, in other children. For these kids, the term *abnormal* included freckles, being overweight, and any obvious signs of intelligence. The problem with those early impressions of "goodness" and "badness" is that they root themselves so deeply in the soil of our psyches and are extremely difficult to dig out. Digging out the false sense of being "better than" is just as arduous and necessary as uprooting the sense of being "worse." But dig we must.

The public revelation of me or anyone else being gay is simply a nonevent, just one fact among many. It's interest as gossip derives entirely from public ignorance and prejudice. Like so much in our media-spun world there's no substance beneath the hype. Unfortunately, at the time of this tabloid blitz I hadn't come to terms with this, and I was a very worried fellow.

As I feared, my agent's phone did stop ringing with job offers and stayed silent for about a year. Because my work was pretty much my life, this extended hiatus also worried me. The only reason my joblessness didn't completely overwhelm me with anxiety was that in the beginning I had no idea my "vacation" would last for twelve months.

To top it all off, Martin split.

A few years earlier we found that we were spending too much time apart as actors and felt that something in the partnership needed to shift in order for it to thrive. We decided that two actors in the family were one too many and agreed that when Martin left his budding career as an actor/singer he would move into producing or at least coproducing my projects. This seemed to be the best solution to having a career as well as a relationship.

Martin had produced our Hawaiian television series *Island Son* quite brilliantly. Both the network executives in Hollywood and all of us in Hawaii thought he was terrific. Martin was also an invaluable producer on *The Bourne Identity* miniseries, so by this time he had proved his salt.

However, established Hollywood executive types are highly resistant to sharing power with relative newcomers. Just prior to my outing I selfishly failed to push hard enough for Martin's inclusion on a couple of new television jobs. He felt I had double-crossed him, and he decided to move from Hawaii to Los Angeles to pursue his own projects independently. Without fully realizing it, I had in my blundering self-involvement pushed Martin away.

So there I was in our big Honolulu house, "disgraced" and out of work, and clearly alone. Obviously it was time for some serious reevaluation of my priorities.

One of the few advantages of the current frantic pace of life is the quick replacement of today's scandal with the next day's "shocking revelation" about somebody else. Apart from my yearlong lack of work, my life continued mostly unchanged: Nobody spit on me in the street, and no one burned crosses on my front lawn. The one really important change was positive: I fully realized that the time had come for me to begin to deal decisively and conclusively with my own deep-seated fears. The tabloid headlines in themselves weren't frightening at all; in fact, they were sort of funny. My problem was my terrified reaction to them. The headlines actually did me a great service by forcing me to finally face and understand and heal my own self-defeating mental stories. As I said, it took me almost a decade with Martin's help to find my way to this simple truth.

So, it was a time of considerable upheaval. The worst part was knowing (even though I didn't want to admit it) that I had carelessly endangered my relationship with Martin. I was still less than fully committed. I wasn't yet willing to go to the mat with him. I still had one foot out the back door, and I felt guilty about it.

It helped that I am good at being on my own. I've spent so much time away from home on film and theater jobs that I've learned to enjoy my own company. During these troubled months, my workaholic nature gave way more easily than I expected to the novel freedom of being able to spend the days pretty much as I pleased. And in my new-found leisure I rediscovered an old friend.

CANVAS, BRUSHES, AND PAINTS

I had done very little painting since my student days at Pomona College, where I had unceremoniously jilted art for acting. But I continued to think about painting a lot, and my "painter's eye" kept spotting beautiful subjects, possible paintings that almost never materialized. Now that I had time on my hands I thought, "Ah hah, why not start painting again."

As the years sail by, the mellow, carefree mai tai and sunset life here in Hawaii becomes less and less resistible. The flower-scented air and the slow rhythms of the surf combine with sweet people and two-finger poi (that yummy gummy pureed taro root) to calm nerves and cool down the hot fires of ambition. Living itself becomes a worthy occupation. While I didn't think yet of retiring, I felt less inclined to prove anything to anybody. I began to think of myself as a sort of beach bum who paints, and occasionally acts.

I set up a minimal art studio in our guest house, bought supplies in various mediums (oils are my home base, but I purchased watercolors, acrylics, and pastels as well) and blithely started in on my first project, a small watercolor called *Heavenly Fish*.

Two surprises were in store. I'd thought of myself as a fairly good painter in college but was shocked at how little painterly technique had survived the years. I had an even better eye now, but little skill. On the positive side I found that my work ethic had strikingly improved. In college if a painting wasn't going well I'd trash it and start something else. Now I seemed willing to work on a picture for weeks if necessary in order to find ways to get it right, to produce a painting that was worth looking at.

Two early paintings in particular became training grounds of endless trial and error and hard-won discovery. I know good painting when I see it; I just didn't know how to do it.

The first was a large, rather academic still life called *Magical Mango* with lots of drapery and some fruit. The drapery had a fish pattern and some of the fish began to swim free into the air. I spent weeks drawing and redrawing, painting and scraping off paint, and painting again and scraping again until I finally got something close to what I wanted. About a year later I added some touches that made it just right.

The second workhorse was a seascape of the view from our beach house called *Maili Blue*. Again I had no idea how to paint water, waves, and clouds, but I plugged away at it endlessly until the picture came to life and began "telling" me what to do. I ended up painting the clouds, the mountains, and the sea in three different styles, since they are three different domains of nature, and the variations worked. Anyway I consider these two paintings my first teachers, and I am very fond of both.

A few years and many paintings later I actually had a one-man show at a gallery on the island of Maui. This sounds provincial, but, believe it or not, Maui is one of the biggest art markets in the world (by the way, I was *not* painting dolphins and whales). The show opened with a wild party and lots of friends. It was rather like opening night of a play with yours truly starring as the brilliant, but fatally avant-garde artiste.

Painting is related to acting in that shape, line, color, and rhythm are intrinsic to both, but the creative process is almost totally different. Acting is done by committee—it's a cocreation with sometimes dozens of other people. Even an actor doing a one-person show relies on writers, producers, directors, lighting designers, stagehands, costumers, and such. In a play or a film the character one creates exists only in relationship with all the other actors; none of you can tell the story alone. And what the other actors are doing at any moment inevitably affects what you will do. Even the stars are part of the ensemble experience—they just get paid more. I find great pleasure and excitement in this teamwork.

Painting on the other hand is done alone; *you're* the boss and the only responsible party. You fill the empty canvas with no one but yourself. However, it's true that when a painting is going well, it takes on its own life and begins to tell *you* who it is and what it needs. Those are my favorite moments in painting—when a kind of silent communion develops between me and the art in progress.

THE FLAME
OF ATTENTION

When I'm painting a picture, I often reach a point where I know something's missing, but I don't know what. I don't know how to proceed. Then I sit back, look at the emerging picture, and wait, simply directing my attention to what's already on the canvas. I may have to move the canvas to various places around the room, different distances, different light, sometimes turning it sideways or upside down. Sooner or later an idea or several ideas pop into my head. And sometimes they *work*!

Where do these ideas come from? What is the source of art, literature, mathematics, and scientific discovery? Mysteries all. But preceding any creation or discovery is *attention*. It is giving our attention that opens the peepholes and great doors of discovery. When I watch the workings of my mind, including those moments of intuitive, inner knowing that we all experience, I see that my attention is in fact who I am. My attention is the focus of my being. Wherever my attention is is where I am. To the extent that I give anything or anyone my attention, to that extent I am giving them myself. I think attention is our primary power, perhaps our only power. Giving someone or something our entire attention, with no preconceived ideas or agendas whatever, is the essence of love.

In both acting and painting I find moments of communion between the creative but limited workings of my thinking and the eternal, unlimited storehouse of the unknown. The wisdom of the unknown responds to my attention. It responds to my interest (and yours) in its own voice and in its own time. There's no way to know what spirit has to say until it says it.

The other day I was driving along the H-2 freeway in Honolulu. Traffic was heavy and slow, and at one point choked to a standstill. To relieve my boredom I looked off toward the mountains, vaguely noticing a random row of coconut palms among some nondescript buildings.

All of a sudden one palm tree caught my attention and I really looked at it, not as just another thing I called a "tree" among many other things of the same name, but as its single self, standing there fanning out its fronds to catch the sunlight and dance with the breeze.

The minute I really saw this tree I felt a subtle connection with it— for a moment we were in each other's lives, that tree and I.

This was the first time I ever realized that there are two distinct and very different ways of seeing our world and the people in it. There is generalized observation, which is heavily reliant on remembered concepts, names, and ideas: oh, there are some palm trees, the sky is cloudy, here comes my friend Sally. In this generalized mode of observation we see our *idea* of the thing more than the thing or person itself. There is a vague kind of seeing, but not much detail and very little contact.

Then there is the connected, relational kind of seeing in which you give the object or person your entire attention. This form of seeing notices the particular tree and what it's doing, it sees the shapes and changing forms of the clouds against the blue sky, it sees how Sally is moving, how she is dressed, what her mood is, and it sees and feels the look in her eyes.

In my experience, general observation, while obviously useful, is remote and uninvolved; you see things and people in a generic sort of way. Its inner feeling is somewhat passive. It is a necessary, but impersonal function of our intellect.

Giving our wholehearted attention, on the other hand, is akin to love. Its inner feeling is expansive, alive, connected. You are suddenly in genuine relationship with the object of your interest. When you give your full attention you automatically give yourself, your spirit and life energy, to the object of your interest. Your attention is the flow of your being. Giving your complete attention is an act of love. The recipient of this flow of your total interest, whether a person or a bird or a book or a tree cannot help but respond, however silently, and share itself with you. I think even your car or computer is not impervious to your good-will.

Painting a picture, or any activity that focuses our entire attention, has mystical implications. Our full attention can bring into being that which was not.

All at once my new friend, painting, had to take a backseat again to make way for yet another creative avenue, and I found myself back at work.

A MUSICAL INTERLUDE

Aside from Sondheim I'm not a fan of musicals. However, just as I was settling into my new role as a painter I was offered the part of Henry Higgins in *My Fair Lady*, that splendidly literate musical adaptation of Bernard Shaw's great play *Pygmalion*. Martin had been in touch with some New York producers who had the rights to the musical, and they teamed up to produce this show together.

This time the problem was not Robert Redford, but Rex Harrison, for whom the musical role was written and who gave us the definitive incarnation of Professor Higgins. Rex Harrison was one of the greatest light comedians of all time, and he played Higgins to perfection. How was I to make this wonderful part my own?

The first few weeks of rehearsal were absolute hell for me. I couldn't escape my memories of Harrison's performance and found myself imitating him and hating myself for being so uncreative. Where was *my* Higgins? I couldn't find him.

The director was entranced by our leading lady and wasn't much help. I struggled through the scenes and brilliant songs quite lost and nearly suicidal. About the middle of the rehearsal period I spent a couple of days so panicked that I became almost catatonic. The director shrugged with incomprehension.

Finally these dire straits triggered some deep survival mechanism within me and my creative juices started to bubble—my own Higgins began to emerge.

We toured *My Fair Lady* all around the country for eight months before opening on Broadway. I was still quite scared the first two weeks of performance but soon began to have fun and really enjoy playing this superb material. We were a hit.

Playing a new city almost every week is a mixed blessing. It's fun discovering the unique character of various parts of the country, getting to know northerners and southerners and westerners in their differing environments. On the other hand, playing eight shows a week and then having to pack up and spend your one day off traveling—often great distances—to the next venue, getting used to the new hotel and new bed and new weather and new theater and backstage crew, can be exhausting.

Boston, where we played a merciful four weeks, was a delightful exception—there was time to settle in and explore that extraordinary city more thoroughly.

One Monday (our day off) I spent a lazy afternoon in my hotel room watching television and then reading a book of Rumi's exquisite poetry. Rumi was a thirteenth-century teacher and mystic who was born in Afghanistan, then part of the Persian Empire, and emigrated with his family to Turkey. As he grew up, Rumi, whose father was also a mystic, fell head over heels in love with the divine. He called the divine his "beloved" and expressed his passionate embrace of the sacred in hundreds of ecstatic poems of great beauty and power.

For a couple of hours that afternoon I sat on my Boston hotel bed quite transfixed by Rumi's songs of divine love and the sublime freedom of unfettered awareness and pure uncaused joy. His expressions of bliss brought tears to my eyes.

Descending from these heights, I ordered a light dinner from room service and decided to see a movie. I'd heard good things about the film *Fried Green Tomatoes,* which was playing nearby, so I pulled on my sneakers and trotted off to see it.

Popcorn and Sprite in hand, I sat down in my theater seat and munched as the previews appeared. When *Tomatoes* started and the rather ordinary characters on-screen began to speak, I was suddenly aware that (I'm not sure how to express this) they were speaking God, that they and their ordinary lives *were* God, were divine.

I glanced around the cinema and saw everyone in it as divine. After the movie, walking back to my hotel, the whole city seemed quietly sacred. As I entered the hotel lobby I spoke to the receptionist and she too glowed with a subtle divinity.

It seemed to me that for a couple of precious hours (thanks to Rumi) I woke up. The veils of my soporific ignorance, which usually mask transcendent reality, were parted slightly by some divine breeze of grace. I was reminded of the Japanese woman praying at the Shinto shrine in Kyoto during *Shogun*. It was a brief, but incalculably precious gift that was absolutely free.

I suspect that such experiences cannot be willed or sought after. The inner openness that makes grace possible is a state beyond thinking, will, and conceptual understanding. It is an openness beyond any image of self. It allows a glimpse of one's true nature, and the sacred nature of the world.

It was during the tour that my mother died. My father had passed away years earlier, after emphysema had reduced him to a kind of cantankerous frailty. Several times during his last weeks Mom and my brother had heard him whisper, "Please take me." Then one afternoon Bill was sitting with Dad in my parents' living room, Dad in his big chair looking out over his beloved view of Laguna Beach and the sea and sky beyond. In a moment of quiet Dad slumped a little and was gone.

Mom was the same age, but she outlasted her husband by about seven years, during which a series of tiny strokes gradually robbed her of her memory. When *My Fair Lady* played Orange County, I visited her at home. She was immobilized in a wheelchair and didn't seem to recognize me at all. I had a feeling this would be the last time I would see this brave woman, who had taken such good care of us. The next day I was to move on with the show back to the East Coast. I hugged her and told her blank eyes that I loved her and that she had been a wonderful mother.

Two weeks later, just before going onstage as Professor Higgins I was told that Mom had died. I thought, given her condition, that this was a blessing. It wasn't until I started singing my last song, "I've Grown Accustomed to Her Face," that the full emotion of the loss finally hit me. All the lyrics seemed suddenly to be about my mother. Somehow I wept my way through the song and finished the show. It seemed like a fitting good-bye to this lovely woman and her difficult life.

About a year after the show closed, Martin produced another production of *My Fair Lady* in Europe. We had reconciled at the end of the American tour. Martin sensed that I had begun to realize that his well-being was at least as important as my own, and thank God, he came back home.

We decided it would be a good idea to create another production for Germany, France, and Switzerland. Our friend Joe Hardy directed this one, and I felt it was far superior to the New York version even though we played huge auditoriums and even sports arenas in various German cities. Many Germans speak English, and they seemed to get most of the jokes and understand the subtleties of British wit.

We also played Zurich and Paris on our tour. The French are not so fond of English, so we had electronic subtitles on each side of the stage to translate our lines into French, causing a very strange delayed reaction problem for us actors. By the time the French audience had read the occasionally funny lines and then laughed, we players were already speaking the next lines onstage. Actors normally wait for laughs to finish before continuing, but how do you wait for a laugh that doesn't come until four or five seconds after the line is spoken? It took us several performances to figure out our timing in this peculiar situation and we never did get it quite right—a comic dilemma for a comedy.

Both of these productions were so successful that two years later I was asked to take over the part of Captain von Trapp in a gorgeous Broadway production of *The Sound of Music*. Mistakenly thinking this was just a sweet show for kids, I was hesitant. Martin and I agreed to fly to New York to take a look, and I was bowled over by its lavish staging and by the show itself, which was much more deeply touching than I'd remembered.

Susan Schulman, the director, had emphasized the frightening aspects of the rise of Nazism in Austria, giving the show added weight and danger. The cast, including Jan Maxwell as Elsa, was for the most part first-rate. Martin joined the production team and asked for certain changes in the show, including one particular bit of miscasting, and the show soared. I even received one of the best reviews of my career from the *New York Times* when we opened. In a musical!

Rehearsing to take over a leading role in an already running show is a bizarre experience. Obviously the show's actors are unavailable, so you're stuck rehearsing with understudies and stage managers. Often the stage manager directs the rehearsals when the actual director is busy elsewhere—often working on yet another show. You must develop your performance in a kind of limbo, hoping against hope that what you're doing will somehow fit into the existing production when the time comes.

I didn't get to play Captain von Trapp with the principal actors on the actual sets until a couple of quick run-throughs the day before I went onstage for real. Again it took me about two weeks of performing to finally settle in.

We played Broadway for several happy months and then ventured off on a ten-month tour of the States. The tour was one of the most successful in history.

Eight performances a week plus constant traveling make touring an endless grind that requires total discipline and the stamina of mountain goats. But our wonderful cast with charming Meg Tolin as Maria saved the day. We all had a lot of fun together despite the arduous schedule.

I was surprised to see, in all this traveling around, how homogenized our country has become. City after city, state after state, the same malls with the same shops and Cineplexes selling the same movies and clothes repeated themselves everywhere. Apart from Boston, Portland, and maybe San Francisco it seemed like we'd keep getting on planes, fly a thousand miles, and then land in the same place.

THE INDEPENDENTS

In and around these theatrical ventures I acted in three incredibly disparate independent feature films. The first was titled *Bird of Prey* and was shot in Sofia, Bulgaria. I played Jennifer Tilly's father and Lesley Ann Warren played my oddly sexy mistress. The lead was a Bulgarian actor who wrote the screenplay to star himself and who seemed to be paying for the entire production with cash literally out of his own pocket. He'd just reach in and pull out wads of what we began to jokingly refer to as Bulgarian Mafia lucre whenever and wherever necessary.

Bulgaria seemed a highly cultured country brought to the edge of ruin by seventy years of Communist domination. The grand buildings of Sofia were charming, but crumbling. Our local film crew was sweet and friendly, but most seemed to have been robbed by their former patriarchal bosses of their ability to take any initiative and get things done. Our sets, for instance, were a shambles, saved only by the skill of our British lighting designer who transformed the dreadful decor with magical light and shadow—mostly shadow.

Gypsies with trained bears were the popular street entertainment. My hotel room overlooked a town square with flower vendors and always at least one of these formerly majestic, now pathetic bears forced by chains linked to their sensitive noses into doing demeaning tricks.

The grand prize of this production was our director, Temi Lopez, a highly talented Venezuelan with a charming accent and considerable flamboyance.

As we began the film we were rehearsing my first scene with Jennifer. Partly because I was still searching for my character, I was relying on my usual overcalculated and preconceived acting style. When we were ready to shoot the scene, Temi took me aside and said a bit plaintively, "Richard, Richard, you are so handsome, so charming, please stop 'acting' and just be yourself."

This was one of those simple, but perfectly timed statements that hit home with a wallop. The seed, "Just be," planted by Nana years before was ready to sprout. If he'd said it a year earlier I might not have understood, but I was somehow ready to hear it and get it and, most important, I was ready to risk. I thought, that sounds exciting, why not! So, more than ever before, I consciously stopped "acting" and started playing around with just being myself as the character and letting it all happen. This new freedom worked like gangbusters and was great fun to boot.

Thanks to Temi I was able to continue this experiment in spontaneity in *A River Made to Drown In,* my second indie film. The director was James Merendino, a precociously gifted child of twenty-something who moved his camera around with astonishingly liquid grace *and* worked well with us actors. We shot the film along a particularly seedy stretch of Santa Monica Boulevard in Los Angeles.

I played a successful and flamboyant lawyer who had had affairs with several male hookers he'd picked up along this notorious street. When he learns that he's dying of AIDS, he returns to his old haunts trying to find the young man he really loved (played by Michael Imperioli of *Sopranos* fame), wanting to leave the kid a legacy of some kind.

Working with Michael (a first-rate actor) and Uta Lemper who played Michael's on-again, off-again girlfriend, and with Merendino and his young, hip crew was a novel treat—my first brush with young Hollywood.

The third film, *The Pavilion,* was based on a Robert Louis Stevenson short story—a period adventure in which I got to play an old cocaine-sniffing scoundrel who was forced out of the slave trade by the American Civil War. He proceeded to swindle the Mexican government out of millions in gold that he hid on a deserted island off the coast of North Carolina. The story involves him, his daughter (Patsy Kensit), with whom he may or may not be sleeping, and his cohort (Craig Scheffer) hiding out in an abandoned pavilion on the island with the vengeful Mexicans in hot pursuit.

I've always thought of myself as a character actor in leading-man clothing, so playing this nefarious codger in all his seedy complexity was a wonderfully freeing challenge. Portraying leading men can be great—they blitz the villains and get the girl—but their parameters are necessarily narrow. The emotional, creative, quirky, and humorous possibilities in playing character parts are much more varied and a lot more fun.

The movie was shot on Bald Head Island off the Carolina coast, an island that the director's father happened to be developing. It was off-season so each actor got to stay in his or her own big house right on the sea where dolphins leapt and played almost every day. One afternoon I saw three dolphins jump in perfect unison high out of the water and dive back in with total perfection, as if they were trained as part of a Sea World entertainment. But they had contrived this amazing stunt on their own, just for fun.

THE THORN BIRDS II

For at least a couple of years during the mid-nineties the Wolper organization, which produced the immensely successful *The Thorn Birds*, was pushing to capitalize on that big-time winner with a sequel, and they kept asking me if I would reprise the role of Father Ralph. Since most of the main characters were either old or dead by the end of the original show, they proposed inventing a new story to fit into a vacant period in the middle of the first saga.

Knowing that sequels, or in this case a mid-quel, usually disappoint, I declined. The producers continued to press until I finally said I would consider playing Ralph again if they came up with a script that at least equaled the excellence of the original. A script finally materialized, but I found it a bit dull compared with what we had already done, and I declined again.

About a year later a high-powered network executive I had worked with and liked when he was a producer called me out of the blue and invited Martin and me to dinner at the Four Seasons in Beverly Hills. It was great to see him again. In the middle of our lively conversation he casually said, "Oh, by the way, did you know that *The Thorn Birds II* is all ready to shoot in Australia, but they still haven't been able to cast a new Father Ralph?" I looked over to Martin and lightbulbs flashed above both our heads.

The next morning I called my agent at Creative Arts Agency (CAA) with this juicy news and said I would agree to play Father Ralph again, but for quite a fantastic salary. I named an impossible figure. Two days later my astonished agent called back and nearly shouted into the phone that they had in desperation agreed to our price. I picked myself up off the floor, packed my bags, and flew to Sydney.

The incomparable Rachel Ward had wisely turned down this dubious project; she was replaced by Amanda Donohoe, also a beautiful and very good actress. But, alas, the chemistry was not the same. As good as the new cast was, it was disconcertingly odd to replay Father Ralph with a new lover, a new son, a new Luke, and a new Cardinal mentor. We all worked very hard to make the show compare as favorably as possible to the original. Whether or not we succeeded I don't know, because I didn't have the heart to look at the finished product. *The Thorn Birds: The Missing Years* was, however, a considerable success in the numbers game.

Along with this surprising variety of jobs and the immense relief of exorcising my demons and making peace with myself, the generous nineties offered me the chance to make peace with the specter of my father.

HATRED AND FORGIVENESS

The person I've hated most often and intensely is my father. It wasn't the only feeling I had for Dad. I was grateful that he worked hard and paid the bills, I respected his common sense in practical matters, and in later years I admired his important work in Alcoholics Anonymous. But mostly I experienced Dad as self-aggrandizing, hypocritical, and covertly, but powerfully, suppressive to all of us, including my mother. I felt subdued and powerless around him. Without physical violence, Dad somehow managed to keep us all scared. Even after he sobered up and became a revered speaker in AA (claiming to have abandoned his ego and to have taken up residence at the right hand of God), I experienced him being sober but otherwise little changed.

Dad's public persona was immensely helpful to hundreds of people in AA. Folks I'd never met used to come up to me in airports and supermarkets and say that my dad had saved their lives. But he could be a very negative presence at home.

Of course I wanted to confront Dad with what I thought were his many offenses, to whittle him down to size and to find my own strength in his presence. But, sensing my fear, he easily demolished my attempts to challenge his power. My failure to stand up to my father only intensified my hatred and my desire for some kind of revenge.

Feeling in some way victimized by a parent is not uncommon. A victim is subjected to oppression, hardship, or mistreatment. Certainly a child, needing care, love, and nurture, can be the victim of oppression and mistreatment and will quite naturally be hurt and angry. But as we mature into independence, is it wise to drag along with us childhood hurts and hates that are no longer relevant to our lives? Is it wise to hold on to negative stories about the love we *should* have gotten and how we *should* have been encouraged and how awfully misunderstood we were? By hanging on to and failing to understand and move on from our past hurts, disappointments, and anger we pollute our present lives. We torture ourselves over and over again not with present facts, but with distant memories, no longer relevant stories. And, given the unreliable and self-serving nature of memory, we can't even be sure these wrongs really happened as we thought they did. And we certainly can't be sure of the "wrongdoer's" motives and intentions. It is simply not possible to fully understand another human being. The only person we can truly know is our self (and *that* takes a lifetime or more).

Believe it or not it wasn't until my late forties that I felt I had the strength and the ammunition to launch an appropriately devastating attack on my father's arrogant and domineering persona. I thought I had at last seen through his Wizard of Oz machinations into the weaknesses and fears that motivated his destructive behavior. I was going to dart in behind his defenses and expose him as a lily-livered fraud.

However, just as I was preparing for all-out war, Dad, a longtime smoker, was enfeebled by emphysema. This once majestic tyrant, now tied to an oxygen tank, could barely walk across his living room. Bloody revenge was out of the question. There would be no satisfaction in punching a dying man. So it seemed as if I'd be stuck with my angry victimhood forever.

That was the delusional soap opera I was living. I actually believed that by changing or wounding my father (showing him the error of his ways in order to improve his behavior or reduce him to rubble), I would at last find my own strength and well-being. Wrong. Once I was grown, the only power my father had over me was power *I* gave him. The source of my well-being as well as the source of my fear were within *me* not him. The only person in our difficult relationship who needed to change was ME. The only solution to my problems of hating and fearing Dad was forgiving him. But how do you *do* that?

Forgiveness is defined as ceasing to feel angry or resentful toward another. I think forgiveness is vastly more than pardoning a wrong. Forgiveness is coming to understand that there is in fact *nothing* to forgive. If I burn my hand in a fire, I don't feel wronged by the flame. Fire is hot—that's a fact, not an offense. If Dad was as oppressive as I thought he was (I cannot be sure), that's simply who he was; his oppression was the result of his own inner dilemmas and like a flame it gave off a dangerous heat, a heat that surely could hurt. But like a flame, my dad's hurting of others was not personal, it was the radiation of his own pain.

It might be argued that fire does not *intend* to hurt, but the person does. Indeed I believe my father *did* intend to suppress his family to retain his secretly fragile dominance. And I think he enjoyed this power. But again, like the flame, that's just who he was. We all were burnt, but we were not wronged. To be wronged implies a *right*, a *should have been*. But *should* is invariably a fantasy. What is *is* what is.

This does not for a second relieve the "wrongdoer" of personal responsibility for his actions. We're all totally responsible for what we think and do at every moment of our lives and must inevitably take the consequences, good or bad, that are the result of our thoughts and actions. The importance of forgiveness is not so much that it absolves the person forgiven as that it cleanses the person who forgives. Wholehearted forgiveness clears the *forgiver* of all the negative stories and baggage that keep him from dealing wisely and effectively with the offending person or group. Forgiveness clears the way for just action, self-protection, and wise change—not revenge.

With elegant and piercing simplicity, James Baldwin wrote the following on the subject of our personal responsibility:

People pay for what they do, and, still more, for what they have
allowed themselves to become. And they pay for it simply: by the
lives they lead.

Dad's behavior had serious consequences. What father *wants* to be
hated and feared by his children? What husband *wants* to drive his wife
into a kind of self-protective somnambulism, creating within her a vol-
cano of anger that didn't surface until he was dying? Excepting his good
works in AA and the somewhat impersonal camaraderie of that group,
Dad was by his own doing frigidly alone. "Nobody knows me, even my
wife doesn't know me," Dad complained to a friend near the end of his
life (as if this was somehow *our* fault). His death in his mid-eighties was
a welcome relief from his long illness. I didn't miss him at all, nor as far
as I know did Bill.

Forgiveness doesn't obviate the need for self-defense. I determined
to be as unlike my father as possible, and I got out of the house, away
from his orbit, as soon as I could. My mother was of course stuck with
him, but even she managed to protect herself by sort of disappearing
behind her charming smile. Bill was stuck working with Dad, but he too
managed to break free after a while.

Yes, we were living with an extraordinarily difficult personality, but
we were not wronged. There he was. It was our job to learn to deal with
him, to survive him. In this life we all have serious, painful challenges.
The trick is to learn to see these difficulties for what they really are and
to handle them with as much wisdom and strength as we can summon
from our hearts and minds, from our friends, advisers, and teachers. If
Mom and Bill and I punished *ourselves* with rancor and resentment,
feelings that have no positive value except as indications that our thinking is off course, that was *our* creation, our doing, not his.

Sure, the rage and revenge we so take for granted as perfectly normal are tremendously stimulating, covertly entertaining, and give us a
deceptive sense of personal power. Witness the horrific and seemingly

endless results of ethnic and religious hatreds around the world, and the excitement of the combatants. Witness the endless soap operas of deceit and vengeance in television and movies. The violence of ill will can become intoxicating, addictive. But these macabre amusements are devoid of the wisdom and joyous freedom of forgiveness.

It is destructive of one's self to wish another human ill. It seems to me that to harm another is to harm God, to harm a variation of one's own self.

The feeling of being wronged comes from our unfounded expectations of being treated fairly, justly, kindly, lovingly, supportively, specially. In the tough and glorious world of what is, we are sometimes treated unfairly, unjustly, even cruelly. Our expectations are often unrealistic, misleading, counterproductive. What is, *is*.

When I am "wronged" I feel pain, then resentment, possibly even hatred for the villain. I wish him ill. What to do in this self-destructive dilemma?

I look at my pain, my hatred, with my whole being. I embrace them as best I can with clear awareness. I try to *see* the "villain" with open-hearted objectivity. He is what he *is*, and he does what he does. His act against me was not (despite appearances) personal any more than earthquakes are personal.

Wholehearted seeing discovers that there is in fact nothing to forgive.

Of course, in some cases the "wrongdoer" should be reprimanded, sued, imprisoned, or some such, but these things can be done out of necessity, without hate, without any personal attachment whatever. Even as he is justly punished, you can wish his spirit well. *Love* has no limits.

If Dad were still alive, I'd tell him with great relief and happiness that the war is over, that I recognize that his spiritual history is unknown to me, and that he lived his troubled life as best he knew how. His integrity is *his* business, not mine. This deep level of forgiveness became real to me several years ago when I was about to be treated for what might have been a serious illness. I asked my dear friends and teachers Carolyn Conger and David Spangler to send me healing energy, a kind of blessing they were both very good at. Carolyn even made me a semihypnotic cassette tape of wonderfully positive thoughts to listen to during treatment.

Well, with their energy flowing my way I glided through this episode as if it were some sort of heavenly party—no fear, no problems, perfect healing. And, as an unexpected bonus, during recovery I was thinking about my troubled relationship with my father and suddenly had a total realization of his complete innocence—the innocence of a rock on which I'd stubbed my toe. He was what he was; there were severe difficulties, but no offense. There was nothing to forgive. My intense, self-destructive resentment evaporated. I at last let go of this exhausting burden.

Just recently this welcome, but somewhat cool understanding of forgiveness in general and of letting go of my father in particular has been greatly deepened and warmed up into love (believe it or not!) by four experiences: a dream, an event, another dream, and a second event, all happening in quick succession. It was obvious to me that these experiences were connected and very important. They happened with a vivid insistence that I attend to them and understand them.

Earlier in the book I mentioned my father's friend, the great metaphysician Ernest Holmes, who founded the Church of Religious Science. Dr. Holmes had visited our home several times, and Dad used to take me to hear his sermons on Sunday mornings. Though I was only ten or twelve at the time and my understanding was limited by youth, some of Dr. Holmes's principles remained in my mind. And my father's philosophy was greatly influenced by Dr. Holmes.

In the first dream I found myself in a spacious building with lots of glass partitions. The building seemed to have aspects of a film set, a library, and the administrative offices of a church. Suddenly, I realized I was in the offices of the Church of Religious Science and I was told that Ernest Holmes was still living and I was directed to his office. I longed to visit him and as I approached his office I saw him through a glass door leaving for the night with an armful of books. Dr. Holmes turned and saw me and exclaimed "Holy shit!" and hurried toward me. We embraced with seemingly equal glee, and a tremendous, vibrant flood of love flowed between us.

The dream sparked my interest in reading Dr. Holmes's work, which I hadn't thought about in years, but I allowed the hurly-burly of my life to distract me. Then a few days after the dream the first "event" happened.

As I was searching through some packing boxes of books in the garage for a certain play I was thinking of doing, I came across a small (in size only) book at the very bottom of the box titled *Ernest Holmes— Seminar Lectures*. I began to read with unexpected excitement. The book was a veritable gusher of wisdom and seemed vibrant with Dr. Holmes's confident presence. As in the dream it was like embracing a beloved friend.

Then came the biggest surprise. While I leafed through the front pages of the book looking for the publishing date I came across this inscription:

Dick,
> *Parts of this book*
> *I find reach the heights.*
> *Most of it in fact.*
> *Let me know how*
> *it strikes you.*
>> *Love,*
>> *Dad*

My father had given me this book perhaps fifty years ago. I had completely forgotten. It was indeed a gift of love. Reading the inscription was almost like hearing Dad's voice speaking to me with warm affection. I could feel his presence all around me.

A few days later I had the second dream. It took place again on a film set, which also seemed like a large cruise ship. I was standing in a big room when the actor Jason Robards (with whom I had worked on a film in England) came up to me with a joyous smile and embraced me in a warm hug, saying he was so glad to see me again. I was equally glad to see Jason and said I thought he was one of the best actors of all time. Again there was complete acceptance and great love between us. Then Jason walked into the ship's bar for some manly festivity.

Whatever else Jason represented in my dream, he was obviously a version of my father. I awoke from the dream with the clear and happy knowledge that I had greatly underestimated my father's capacity for love. And I discovered that despite (and perhaps because of) all our problems and misunderstandings, I loved my father unreservedly, and somehow in spirit he loved me, too.

This was a considerable change from the neutral feeling of forgiveness and well-wishing toward my father that I had come to earlier. This was an active sense of mutually loving friendship.

The second event happened three days after the second dream. I had flown to Los Angeles for a job and was sitting in my hotel room surfing through the TV channels. I happened upon a movie in which Jason Robards played the estranged father of a young woman. He had years before abandoned his daughter and her son to pursue a string of dubious business ventures. At the beginning of the movie the secretly ill Robards character returns to his daughter's home hoping to win back her love and the love of his grandson before he dies. The daughter resists angrily and the boy is suspicious.

Watching the great Robards gradually win over his daughter and especially his grandson with his superb warmth, charm, and honesty, I experienced a kind of spiritual reunion with my own father (the fictional story and my real story happening simultaneously). I fully realized a mutual love between Dad and me that brought tears of gratitude. Our war had ended several years before. Now our peace was filled with joy.

In this new sense of love there is a lightness and freedom which I cherish. Perhaps on a soul level my father and I have always loved each other and had participated in our thorny relationship as a process of mutual teaching and learning. In any case, I sense the warmth of his presence now and feel on some level that we are and always have been true friends.

WHAT IS HATRED ANYWAY?

Some time ago I found myself hating my contractor (whom I had paid top dollar) for screwing up my new house. Being uncomfortable with this negative feeling, I took a long and honest look at the situation. I saw that from the start I had let clues and warning signs slip by; that I had not received enough expert advice along the way; that I had obviously trusted unwisely; that I had not coolly confronted the man and intelligently discussed the situation either during construction or before instituting legal means to demand restitution. From the beginning, I hadn't dealt wisely with the problem.

In short, hatred is nothing more than our immature avoidance of dealing with reality; it is stimulating but useless. Hatred totally shuts out love, and love is the smartest thing there is. Everything else is dumber than love. Children escape into hatred. Grown-ups size up the dilemma, acknowledge their complicity, summon all their smarts, and, if need be, all their professional advisers, and *deal with the realities,* without the distractions of rancor.

And here's yet another of life's cosmic jokes. Our negative thoughts and feelings are self-created and exist only in our heads, not out there in the world. The world simply is what it is. We're the ones who choose a negative stance. The world at any present moment is exactly as it should be, there being no alternative. Spilt milk cannot be unspilt. The question is, do we cry and moan about it or do we clean it up and be more careful the next time? Time can't be reversed. We cannot change the present moment, but we can certainly change the next one. And we can certainly change our thinking. Wouldn't it be dumbfounding to discover that *all* negative feelings are in fact dispensable?!

THE TWENTY-FIRST
CENTURY AND YET
ANOTHER REINVENTION

By the time this book is published I'll be, amazingly, sixty-nine years old. The trappings of youth are long gone, and the subtractions of age have begun. Though acting still fascinates me, the glory days of my once all-important career are over. The infamous paparazzi are looking elsewhere for their thrills.

When I was growing up, the middle-aged and elderly people seemed to feel it was quite natural and right for them to be middle-aged and elderly. Youth, with all its excitements and confusions, was something to get over, not a place in which to linger or to cling to. Middle age, with its house and job and kids, was where life happened, and old age was a fitting denouement.

In movie dramas and love stories of the thirties and forties, the actors were predominately mature, fully grown, made interesting and desirable and glamorous by their life experience rather than by pimples and raging hormones. Even the child actors in those films were often un-cute and middle-ageish. Youth was considered slightly annoying.

The British pushed the point even further: They rarely saw their children until they returned from boarding school and university with doctorates in hand.

Not so today.

I suspect that our current worship of callow youth and its frivolities and our panic in the face of the wrinkles of experience are signs of considerable cultural decadence. Grown-ups are passé.

Though I admire maturity in others, I reluctantly admit to having been seriously addicted to youth. As a beginning actor I was secretly certain that my success was almost entirely due to my youthful good looks; that when my youth waned, so would I.

Luckily, my parents passed along hardy genes and my youthfulness lasted an astonishingly long time. I don't remember feeling or looking older until I was well up into my fifties.

It has long been rumored that I have had several face-lifts. In Hollywood everyone past the ancient age of twenty-nine is suspect. For years I took this chatter as a sort of compliment, but being disbelieved is never pleasant.

When I was touring Europe in *My Fair Lady,* we held a press conference in Hamburg where the reporters' questions were particularly invasive on several subjects, one being cosmetic surgery. Exasperated by their persistence, I offered this challenge: Bring in a respectable plastic surgeon to examine me closely. If he finds a single bit of evidence (inevitable scarring) of any "lifting," I will pay you ten thousand dollars cash. If he finds no signs of surgery, you may pay *me* the ten thousand dollars cash.

I repeated this offer on Larry King's show when he asked if I had "had any work done." The offer still stands. So far there have been no takers.

Because of this preternatural extension of youthfulness, the long-delayed but inevitable ravages of time have taken me completely by surprise. My life is morphing into something quite different and new. Who am I? What am I becoming? It seems to be time for another reinvention.

Fortunately, as I gaze into my still somewhat murky crystal ball I glimpse some happy prospects.

Caressed by balmy trade winds, and the sea's amiable warmth, the enchantment of living in Hawaii way out here in the middle of the Pacific Ocean—unlike youth—has never waned. I'm still fascinated with and challenged by my painting, and acting continues its allure. I still feel the excitement of beginning a new job with new actors and crews, and a unique character to find and create. But sitting around shooting the breeze with friends or walking the dog along a palmy beach are pretty great, too!

The one consistency underlying all these possibilities is my keen interest in the endlessly mysterious pas de deux of body and spirit, of the seen and the unseen, of time and eternity, of fiction and truth.

I love to think about life. I love to listen to life. And I feel that the unseen aspects of creation love to be attended to, and questioned by, us visible beings. If properly listened to I think the invisible will answer us in its own time with its own insightful voice. The great trick on our part is of course learning to listen.

A LETTER
CONCERNING SELF

Writing this book has made me think more deeply about our morphing world and has helped to open a new phase in my life. Carolyn Conger and David Spangler, spiritual teachers and dear friends of mine, have each asked me to participate with them in teaching various student groups they work with. Though I certainly do not consider myself an authority of any kind, I love this experience of discussing with serious students the possibilities of stepping beyond the limitations of our conditioned thinking and opening ourselves to the wisdom and power of love despite all the craziness dancing around our planet.

David Spangler recently asked me to coteach a workshop of his in Seattle titled "Standing Within Self." I said that I'd welcome the challenge, and he asked me to write down a few of my thoughts on the subject of self and send them to him. I sat down and wrote the following letter.

Dear David,

"Standing Within Self" seems a perfect subject. As a person who has feared and rejected himself for decades and pretended to be a more acceptable someone else, and who has only recently (at age sixty-eight!) discovered a place of truth within and found the joy of trusting that wellspring, the various levels of self are a subject I'd love to explore with you and your students.

The word "self" refers to so many states of being. Krishnamurti said the self is nothing—I agree. I also think the self can expand into everything. I also think the self is God's (that is, all of life's) laboratory of discovery—each self is an aspect of God learning.

I'm currently very interested in detachment. It seems obvious that clear awareness, compassion, and love presuppose detachment. I've only begun to think about this. What detaches from what? The self as most of us experience it is the very bastion of attachment, need, want and desire. Self-protection and survival and self-exploitation are paramount. And we accept the various fictions of our self-image as the real thing. Detachment is thought to be cold, even a kind of death. And of course it is a kind of death, and there lies its beauty. Detachment dies to the old as it innocently approaches the new.

So here we are, alternatively manufacturing the self, exploiting the self, fictionalizing the self, plumbing the self, deepening the self, losing the self, finding the self, and searching out the self divine.

Yes we're separate, yes we're one, yes we're profane, yes we're sacred, yes some are smart and some are dumb, yes we share the same Mind and very likely, the same soul.

Krishnamurti asks profoundly, disturbingly, "When thought ceases, where is the self?"

Is the self entirely the product, the projection of thought? If thought precedes self, who is thinking?

I suspect that the only thing that thinks is God (the essence of all that is). Life is thinking us, life is breathing us, life is learning us. We are the instant manifestation of God's thought. God's thoughts are not abstractions like ours, God's thoughts are the thing (mountain, star, bird, person) itself. God thinks abstractly through Itself as us.

How elusive and various the self can be. In one day, one hour,

*I can be depressingly cynical and joyfully inspired, grumpily list-
less and vitally engaged. Our self is naturally so liquid and quick,
yet we're frightened of change, of the new, so we tie ourselves down
and nail ourselves to an image, a collection of past ideas. We
deaden ourselves with comfortable sameness. Or, finally bored to
death by such predictability, we wake up and let go and let life
fling itself into us.*

    *Then, as you have said, David, our elastic self can expand
from its separate nucleus into great things.*

Love,

Richard

I co-led the two-day workshop with David in Seattle in which we
explored many aspects of the thing we call "self." The group included
about thirty people, nearly all of whom seemed smart and eager to learn.
The great thing about teaching—especially for a novice like myself—is
that you learn so much by doing it. We met all day Saturday and Sunday
in a large yurt at Moss Hollow, a rustic mountain retreat outside of Seattle. David usually introduced the topic of the morning or the afternoon
sessions, and then I would chime in with my ideas and experiences. A
group discussion followed. I was struck by the vitality of these discus-
sions. The mostly middle-aged participants were thoughtful and wise
and deeply committed to enriching their experience of life and spirit.

    After finishing David's workshop, I flew down to Los Angeles and
worked with one of Carolyn Conger's ongoing groups. This smaller
group of women from all around the country meets with Carolyn four
or five times a year. Because they've all studied together for so long,
these women shared a depth of understanding and cocreative energy
that brought out the best in all of us. My subject in our two-hour session was the stupendous power and intelligence of love, including forgiveness and the overrated dramas of negative thinking. Again, I
learned as much from them as they did from me.

I had assisted both David and Carolyn in their workshops before, and together with writing this book, I do seem to be morphing into something new. My desperate need for fame and prestige is giving way to the realization that the emptiness I so feared is actually vibrant with the silent treasures of spirit. Like everyone else, the love I sought from the outside is always abundantly present within my own being. The object isn't to "get" love, but to share the love we already have.

DEPENDENCY, FEAR,
AND HAPPINESS

One night I was quite tired when I went to bed and expected to fall asleep easily. The night was cool and silent, the bed soft and enfolding. Oblivion beckoned pleasantly. But I started thinking about a business problem, a confrontation concerning an unfair contract that I'd scheduled for the morning. Immediately I felt confused, anxious, and fearful. The possibility of sleep vanished.

So I switched on the light and picked up the nearest book, which happened to be *The Impossible Question* by J. Krishnamurti. I opened it and found by happy chance a discussion of fear and the process of self-awareness.

Krishnamurti was describing each individual life as swiftly alive, ever changing, vital, always new. Our fixed self-image is an idea, a concept, not the real thing. Knowing one's self is not a matter of accumulating knowledge as memory, which is always of the past, but of deeply observing one's self right now, of seeing who we are each moment.

He suggested to his listeners (which included me as I was reading) that we look at our fear—not our memories of fear or our ideas about fear, but whatever fears we feel at this very moment—and that we look into the effects of our present fear and also its causes.

So I quit dithering about the imminent confrontation with this greedy producer and did just that. It was immediately apparent to me that I was intimidated by the necessity of dealing with this overbearing guy and his one-sided contract because I hadn't yet clearly thought out the deal I wanted. I was feeling victimized by a document that I now realized I had the power to rewrite according to my needs. I went to my office, typed up a statement of terms I thought were fair to both parties, and returned to the warmth of my bed with a quiet mind. Sleep was sweet. The next day we both signed *my* version of the contract.

This is an example of dealing sensibly with a particular instance of fear. Dealing with the whole question of fear requires deeper inquiry.

Threats to one's physical survival—the hiss of a poisonous snake, being awakened by the smell of smoke, an onrushing truck—engender fears that are natural and vital. They provoke immediate action.

Or almost immediate. Once I was playing the part of Frederick Cook in a television movie about the race of Cook and Peary to be the first man to discover the North Pole (Rod Steiger played Peary). We were shooting the film in northern Canada.

One crystal-clear, frigid day we were filming scenes driving dog sleds on a vast five-hundred-acre island of floating ice. The amazing sled dogs were stealing the show and all was going well when suddenly there was an unearthly sound of crackling, sliding thunder and our bright white ice island slowly, gracefully broke in half. The large crew, vehicles, cameras, and sound equipment were on one half and the actors and dog teams on the other.

As I watched in awe as these two enormous plains of ice slowly drifted apart, I was still in the fantasyland of acting, and my first reaction was a kind of wonder at the terrific special effects moviemakers could contrive. Then I noticed the magical beauty of the brilliant green colors of the submerged areas of ice against the black arctic water. Finally the mad and barely successful dash of the dogs and sleds charging over the widening gap woke me up to the reality and danger of the situation. Without thinking my adrenaline-charged body leapt across the broad abyss of freezing water like a champion broad jumper. Fear triumphed—I made it.

Psychological, spiritual fear is quite another matter. Fearfulness, which is not the result of actual physical danger, is nearly always caused by our attaching our happiness to someone or something. This could be to a lover, money, beliefs, social position, home, Porsche, job, husband or wife—whatever we believe is necessary for our well-being. Any attachment creates dependency (my happiness depends on your love, your approval—my-well being depends on my wealth, my power, my youth or status). Any dependency invariably opens us to the fear of loss. Where there is attachment, there is dependency. Where there is dependency, there is fear.

The obvious truth of this dependency-fear equation brings up an astonishing question. Is there such a thing as unconditional happiness? We're so used to being emotionally dependent that the very idea sounds loony. It seems laughably impossible to even imagine a way of living, a state of being that is emotionally and spiritually independent of desire, possession, control, security, and habit—a way of living that is utterly free and full of spontaneous uncaused joy. But isn't that exactly what love really is?

Of course we depend on thousands of people for thousands of things: the trash collectors, the sewage plant operators, the farmers, the truckers, the schoolteachers, and all the people and machines that make our physical lives possible. When our survival is threatened, naturally we're afraid.

But psychological, emotional, and spiritual dependency is another kettle of squid. As long as I attach my happiness, my well-being to fame or applause or good reviews or even big paychecks, I'm in trouble. All these things come and go. As long as my well-being depends on your love I'm in trouble. Personal love can be fickle, it comes and goes. And if my happiness depends on your loving me, my love for you will subtly take a backseat to my need to possess and control you.

This is my case for detachment. Detachment is usually thought to be cool and distant. It is in fact the opposite. When I am attached to you, I must hang on to you and manipulate you so you'll stay around—that's what makes me cool and distant. When my source of happiness is within myself, only then can I appreciate and love you unreservedly, only then can I set you free. When I'm with you the music is beautiful; when I am alone the music is still beautiful, just a different melody, a different rhythm.

Detachment and happiness and love are the best of friends.

THE ONLY THING TO DO

Idly flipping through TV channels one afternoon, I came across a public access program featuring a youngish guru type expounding Eastern philosophy. We'll call her G. She seemed to me too attractive; too, well, ordinary and down-home American, too pretty and sunny to be taken seriously as a teacher, but something kept me watching.

G. was speaking to a large group of mostly young people who seemed utterly enraptured by her. I found their enthrallment suspect, as if they had abandoned themselves, their independence, to her glow.

And glow she did. As I watched I could see that G. was richly gifted (she was the student of some high-powered Indian gurus) with a profound serenity enlivened by keen intelligence. When she interacted with members of her audience, she was fully present for them, fully engaged with them. I began to fall under her spell.

I sent in for some of her videos and was so impressed and enraptured by her teaching that I flew to the mainland to attend several of her meetings. Actually being in G.'s presence was indeed a heady experience, but I began to feel an important limitation in her work. She was able to invoke a state of bliss in her gatherings that I thought was somewhat like a drug in that it was hugely pleasant, but, as far as I could tell, had little or no relevance to one's daily life.

I think one's religion, one's spiritual life, is not a matter of beliefs and theologies. One's religion is the way one lives day to day. One's spiritual life is the way one relates to one's fellow beings and to one's self.

Ultimately one's religion is simply awareness of what is—awareness being an invitation to the action of love.

It seemed to me that G.'s avenue to bliss was in fact an alluring escape from a mature understanding of the reality of exactly who and what one is in the present moment, an escape from seeing what *is*. So, with a touch of regret, I lost interest in her teachings.

A couple of years later I was again idly surfing through TV channels when I happened onto the final moments of yet another G. video. G. was working with a handsome young woman who complained of the frustration of her fruitless search for inner peace and enlightenment. All her efforts toward the divine ended in failure and continuing unhappiness.

With radiant calm, G. pointed out the fact that concepts of enlightenment, of God, no matter how beautifully thought out, are never the thing itself. Consequently chasing after concepts, however magical they may seem, is chasing after illusion. Enlightenment is always new and only now. It can never be captured and held by thought. Thought, ideas, are always the response of memory, which is obviously always an accumulation of the past.

G. then suggested that the young woman stop all searching for some ideal fantasy beyond herself and instead turn her entire attention to the present facts of her inner state of being at that moment. If she was feeling frustrated, unhappy, and lost, then embrace those actual feelings with her entire awareness. G. encouraged her to delve into her present state of being not intellectually, but by allowing the loving intelligence of total awareness to penetrate to the very core of her present suffering. G. suggested that this total awareness leave behind all desire for change, all likes and dislikes, all judgments of good or bad that cloud clear seeing. Just look at what is. This clear awareness is itself action. It is the gateway to understanding, which is the opening to effortless change. Clear, clean awareness is a profound aspect of love and an utterly natural window to the divine.

The young woman tapped into this beautiful understanding, as did

G., as did I watching. This is sometimes called an altered state of consciousness, because it's so unlike our "normal" state of highly conditioned thought. But when you touch this silent awareness, it seems supremely normal, absolutely right, utterly clear and whole. It is vibrant with a kind of clear, nonverbal intelligence, a knowing beyond knowledge. It is indescribable in words, but essential to living wholly, without conflict. It is truly our home. The handsome young women found truth right in the middle of her frustration.

Whatever I had thought missing in G.'s teaching was now abundantly present. It seems to me that clear awareness is the pathway to the personal transformation that will in turn begin to transform our world. Keeping the eyes of our soul—our awareness—wide open requires constant attention.

Even when we experience occasional moments of awareness, of being awake, the dominance of comfy sleep returns to pretty much rule our lives. My dear and longtime friend Sarah is a physical therapist of uncommon ability. She is highly trained and has immense knowledge of the human body as well as its psychological mysteries. Her learned skills are vast, and when working with her clients, Sarah taps into a level of intuition and wisdom that transforms her learning into an ability to heal far beyond mere knowledge. As she accelerates her clients' physical healing, she offers acutely perceptive suggestions concerning how their lifestyle and thinking might change to restore their health and well-being.

While working, Sarah is clear as a bell. The rest of her life, however, has been a bit of a mess. Her professional maturity tends to ebb in her daily life, which is at times fraught with conflict, indecision, and self-defeating stories. She often becomes a little girl avoiding responsibility for practical matters and her personal growth.

Until recently, Sarah smoked around ten cigarettes a day. Intellectually she knew smoking was harmful and was a pretty stupid thing to do. When I suggested that she quit like the rest of us (I smoked until about twenty-five years ago), she said: "Yeah, I know I should, but I'll gain weight if I quit and besides you don't seem to understand that I'm a much more addictive personality than you [do you see the fictional stories here?], so I just can't."

Then came the big shock—Sarah discovered a small lump in her breast that was diagnosed as malignant. It was successfully removed, but her doctor told her that smoking could have contributed.

Well, Sarah's factual, conceptual knowledge about the dangers of smoking suddenly expanded into awareness. All at once she knew deep inside, beyond all rationalizations, that she was dealing with a life-and-death situation. She woke up. She quit.

Sarah is an example of how strenuously even smart people resist awareness when our lazily habitual thought patterns, our usual ways of getting by, our precious fictions and addictions, are threatened.

We're all ensnared by the gravity of the imagined safety of the familiar. We all hesitate to venture into the unknown, into levels of living beyond memory, beyond recognition, beyond the past. Life, love, wisdom, spirit, God—all are always new, now, fresh, never to be repeated. When, in the sleep of the known, we miss the fresh newness of the unknown *now*, we miss that new moment forever.

The past is gone, the future can only be imagined. We humans are swift. We are ever-changing and evolving. We learn at every moment. Discovering the joy, the intensity, the silence, and the freedom of the eternal present requires our full attention and the courage to see what is and to welcome change, the surprise of the new, the passion of living.

THE BEAUTY OF
BREATHING

One way I cope with the alarming aspects of this newish century with some equanimity comes from something incredibly familiar. Breathing. Breathing life-giving air in and out of my lungs is the activity I'll be doing most constantly during the entire length of my physical existence. My heart beats even more often than I breathe, but I can't really be said to beat my heart—that stalwart muscle is happily beyond my control. Breathing, though semiautomatic, is an action I can perform at will with various rhythms and depths.

The life-giving molecular substances of air are created by and are part of the entire universe. Just like the composition of our bodies, air is (for want of a more original word) stardust. We are so used to the constant action of breathing and we take it so for granted that we seldom astonish ourselves with the realization that we are breathing the universe. Our breathing is absorbing life from the stars.

Since matter and energy have been shown by no lesser a gent than Albert Einstein to be interchangeable, and since my basic proposition is that there is nothing but God, it seems likely that everything (stones, molecules, quarks and all) is full of spirit.

Naturally we're going to spend ninety percent of our time being far too busy with the swirl of life to think much about breathing. But somewhere in the remaining ten percent it's wonderful to sit down in a quiet place (if you can find one) and focus on the miracle of breathing.

Try this. Sitting comfortably and alert, breathe in slowly and deeply, pause a second, then exhale slowly and pause briefly. Give your breath your complete attention. Not only is this simple act of breathing an effective way to calm the mind, with a little imagination it can become an art form. Imagine, for instance, that you are breathing divine love into your whole being, and then exhale the warmth of this love into your home or family or into the great oneness of humanity. Or, if you're ill, inhale the vibrant healing energies of spirit, of the angels, and exhale this beautiful energy into your environment. Breathe silence into emptiness, exhale nothingness into nothing. Disappear and discover. Breathe eternity. Whatever we focus our entire attention on tends to bloom and deepen and open to us. Attention is love, and love invites loving response. Even pain and stress, conflict and hostility will share their secrets with love.

Breathe love into a problem and gently ask for solutions. Breathe love into a relationship and see without any expectation what unfolds (or doesn't).

I'm sitting in my study high up in the hills above Honolulu writing and listening to the songbirds that are extramelodious during these early days of spring. Their music lilts into the room on a cool breeze that I inhale and make part of me. Who knows, I may be breathing in some of the very same air these chatty birds just musically exhaled. Breathing birdsong.

ON GLIMPSING
ONE'S SOUL

Several days ago a friend in New York sent me several books by Andrew Harvey. I began to read Harvey's *The Direct Path to God*, in which he describes three experiences that opened him to the mystical aspects of his life. One of these was a vivid dream in which Harvey sat on a beach as a golden androgynous being walked toward him radiant with compassion. The being sat in his lap and a great love flowed between them. Awestruck, Harvey asked the magnificent entity who it was and it replied, "I am you." In the dream Harvey was seeing the loving divinity of his own soul. I found this vision deeply touching.

The next day I was amazed to receive from a fan I'd never met a videotape of the first four television shows I'd ever acted in, dating from around 1959 to 1960. This was especially surprising because I'd just been writing about these same shows in this book.

I watched the tape the following morning with some apprehension. I wasn't sure I wanted to revisit those early days when I had to work so hard to disguise my fears. As I watched the episode of *Gunsmoke*, my first job in television, it was painful to see how emotionally tied up I was beneath the performance. I could see it in certain facial tensions and in the way I moved around as if there were a huge invisible weight on my shoulders. (A writer friend once said watching my early performances was like watching a gazelle caught in a net.)

But despite these inhibitions I was astonished to see the radiance of a beautiful innocence and clarity shining in and around me. It was like seeing two people intertwined—one luminously beautiful and the other tied up in knots. I could see this duel presence only in the first two shows. Then it disappeared.

That evening I was thinking about Andrew Harvey's dream and was suddenly struck by a moving insight. Perhaps, like Harvey, I had glimpsed my own soul. Perhaps each of us is in fact a sacred, radiant presence that has assumed whatever distortions and travails we experience in this life in order to explore and more fully understand and appreciate the nature of its own divinity.

The concept of a divine soul is ancient and so familiar we often take it for granted. But there's a world of difference between a concept and the actual mystical experience of one's spirit. By daring to say that I might have glimpsed the light of my own soul, I'm suggesting the possibility that each of us will at some point be invited by life to delve into the sacred depths of his or her own being. There is great importance in recognizing and exploring this possibility. Imagine coming to know the golden being that is you.

ON MONEY AND SPIRIT

If a genie sprang forth from my cocktail shaker and offered me the choice between enlightenment and a billion dollars tax free, there would be a telltale pause.

I liked being four years old. Life was play, responsibility was an unsuspected bogeyman hiding somewhere in the future. Though I'm sure there were some parental do's and don'ts, very little was expected of me; I felt free to do pretty much as I pleased. It had not yet occurred to me to be anything other than myself. Life was full of new discoveries and wonder. My fourth year was (in memory at least) a time of delightful, quasi-infantile nirvana.

In my daydreams, being filthy rich would be an amplified version of this preschool bliss: unlimited play, adventure, ease, freedom, society and solitude, travel, luxury, simplicity, and, best of all, *security*. Pretense would be passé, worry a pain barely remembered. There would be endless toys: celebrated paintings and sculptures, a yacht, maybe a private jet, splendid travel, a superb chef. And if there was ever any annoyance or pain, there would be too many exquisite amusements to notice. Of course there would be a generous charitable foundation to satisfy my virtuous urges and to assuage the guilt of having so much more than everyone else. I would be in total control. Life would be whatever I wanted it to be.

On the other hand there's enlightenment. How does that compare in my daydreams?

Enlightenment, to use David Spangler's cumbersome but perfect word, is to be *unobstructed,* to at last open one's entire being each moment to the light of intelligence and love, which is intrinsic to our universe, to every atom of what is. It is to discover that beneficent light echoed uniquely in one's self and then to radiate love into our world and *act* with love's wisdom. It is to be willing to throw yourself like a handful of beads up into the cosmos, knowing that you are hurling love into love, knowing that your self, whether reassembled or dispersed in light, will be of service to the divine. It is to abandon the illusion of *security* for the joy of discovering the magnificence of each moment, here and now, just as it is.

Enlightenment is clear, clean awareness unobstructed by all our social conditioning and learned prejudice. This open awareness is itself the action that brings positive change. For the enlightened, the rewards and punishments of heaven and hell have no meaning whatever; you do good for no reason simply because you *are* good. You love simply because you *are* love. You are one with the whole of life.

Beneath all the fun and frolic in my fantasy of great wealth I see an immaturity, an avoidance of life, an orgy of *having* instead of *being.* And endless distraction. It is said that these days we're distracted from distraction by distraction. There is a substitution of material security for a deeper, heartfelt trust in the loving nature of creation. There is a worldly sense of control instead of an open attention to the subtle urgings of the divine. Self-discovery, the very essence of a life worth living, would become the only unaffordable luxury. Sorry, soul, no time for *that!*

So with only a twinge of regret, I would defy the conventional wisdom of our curious culture and choose enlightenment. Love is priceless.

Of course, a more generous genie could offer both kinds of riches: a billion bucks *and* enlightenment; the two are not mutually exclusive. Money, after all, is just condensed energy waiting to do our bidding. Spirit would spend money beatifically.

DREW CAREY

In 2002, I became involved in a real gender-bender on *The Drew Carey Show*, the television sitcom. It all started in the sleepy rural beach town where I live. I was enjoying a shiatsu massage given by an expert local Portuguese woman with blue eye shadow and an extravagant beehive hairdo in her cluttered little office across from the beach.

Several months prior, my exotic masseuse had rescued a mynah bird that had fallen from its nest. This feathered creature had subsequently grown up in a cage and had learned to talk. About halfway through my treatment the silence was abruptly broken by the mynah, saying in its strangely sophisticated and ironically camp voice, "I love papaya . . . I loooooooove papaya . . . I love yoooooooooooooooooooou!! Ha ha ha."

Well, I nearly fell off the massage table laughing.

That week I learned to imitate the mynah's voice and related its slightly insane words to any friends who would listen. They all laughed. Using my imitation of the bird's voice, I discovered a very funny and often witty character who would occasionally "appear" and make amusing comments on whatever was going on. I named her Daphne Papaya. These unpredictable appearances of Daphne seemed to release in me an incisive observation, and a wicked humor that I would never dare express as myself. Where I am cautious and polite, Daphne is fearless and funny.

Playing comedy is extremely difficult, but great fun. Thinking the character had real possibilities, Martin and I wrote a sitcom script starring Daphne and her former-cowboyesque husband, in which I would play both parts. I had never attempted this sort of writing before, but to my surprise the script turned out quite well.

Martin wasn't convinced that I had the *cojones* to play a woman for a short stint, let alone a full season. He challenged me to dress up in full Daphne regalia for a night on the town. I had never dressed in drag before, not because I was fearful of the repercussions, but because it just didn't interest me. Yet the idea of playing Daphne was so exhilarating I felt this could be an opportunity for my expansion into comedy and a new personal freedom.

Running around Honolulu looking for the right wig, the right high heels, and the right gown for the soiree was an eye-opener. When I bought the bra, I had to explain to the saleswoman's arched eyebrows that it was for a reading of a new play. Sitting in a beauty salon having a woman's wig styled on my head summoned up a new kind of courage. When finally done up, I thought I looked fairly glamorous in a slightly off-kilter sort of way, and a tad like my mother, albeit a head taller in those heels.

We invited two close friends to join us for dinner at a very posh Waikiki restaurant that we had never frequented in order to remain as incognito as possible. I was having great fun with this novel acting challenge and the excitement of breaking taboos—until I inadvertently began ordering my meal in my real voice. Martin shot me a stunned look, which startled me right back into character. The maître d' didn't bat an eyelid. As my escort, Martin seemed more uncomfortable than the rest of us. I guess he'd never been out on a date with a transvestite.

After the success of our dinner, I felt ready to venture into television as Daphne Papaya, raconteur, and wickedly witty purveyor of truth.

Martin and I flew to New York to pitch the sitcom idea to my agent and several agency bigwigs. After telling the story idea, I gave them a sample of Daphne's wacky character and voice.

Only my lead agent—and, by the way, possibly the only certifiably straight man in the room—loved the concept. All the others were horrified. "Our romantic hero playing a woman!!! This will ruin your career!" At our insistence the agency said that they would present our idea to various networks and cable channels, but nothing materialized, and the venture languished. Soon thereafter, most of the agents were fired in an agency shake-up. Perhaps they needed a few more *cojones*.

About a year later, my new agent, who knew about our Daphne sitcom, called and said *The Drew Carey Show* was looking for a man to play Carey's boss's mother, Mrs. Wick. Would I be interested in giving Daphne a whirl? Despite my otherwise cautious nature, I love breaking rules—especially arbitrary ones—and I leapt at the chance.

Following in the tracks of Dustin Hoffman and Robin Williams, I was hardly breaking new ground. But the novelty of choosing dresses and jewelry, trying on wigs and makeup, and wearing a padded brassiere and high-heeled shoes in this professional situation was truly weird. There are so many unconscious anxieties and taboos lurking around gender identification that crossing the immense barrier between man things and woman things is hazardous. Years ago Robert Mitchum acted in a movie on location in a penitentiary. Before shooting his scene the makeup person walked up to Mitchum and patted his face with a powder puff (definitely a woman thing) and nearly caused a prison riot. Nevertheless, I loved this Daphne character for her wit and honesty, so I forged ahead.

The *Carey* script, which arrived after I had departed Hawaii for Los Angeles to film the show, was a disappointment. Mrs. Wick lacked Daphne's sophistication and devilish way with words, but Drew and all the actors and producers and crew were bright and friendly, and we had a great time together. And even without Daphne's class, Mrs. Wick got a lot of laughs.

AWARENESS,
CLEAR AND CLEAN

Since my early twenties I've been drawn to the writings of J. Krishnamurti, a spiritual teacher of great purity and renown.

As a boy Krishnamurti was found on a beach in India by members of Britain's Theosophical Society who were searching for the new World Teacher, the new Christ. He was taken to England and intensely trained for this august position. After years of study Krishnamurti was to speak to a large gathering of Theosophists proclaiming his "divinity." He shocked his worshipful audience with his now famous statement that Truth is a pathless land. He denied the value of spiritual authority of any kind, urging everyone present to discover truth for themselves. Truth cannot be learned from another. The profound paradox of a World Teacher is that he/she comes to teach that which cannot be taught. No one can find your heart and soul but you.

I met Krishnamurti twice, first at a television studio where I was in a small audience for one of his rare TV interviews. After the interview, which was very serious, I was totally surprised when Krishnamurti came up to me and took my hand with the spontaneous joy of a child and said he had seen my performance of Thomas Mendip in Christopher Fry's *The Lady's Not for Burning* in Chichester, England, a few years earlier. I was both dumbfounded and delighted.

Some years later, perhaps because of that chance meeting, I was asked to narrate a documentary about Krishnamurti and his teaching around the world.

Shortly thereafter I was invited to attend a small luncheon for Krishnamurti in Ojai, California, where he often gave talks. There were twelve people, and I was seated just across the table from this extraordinary man.

During lunch I asked him a question about his statement that the first step is the last step. He put his hand on my arm and asked with great intensity if I was serious. I said I was. And he proceeded to give me an explanation that seemed to me oversimplified and rote. I was strangely disappointed (expectations making trouble).

As I was leaving to drive home to L.A., the lovely woman who had invited me to the luncheon gave me Krishnamurti's latest book called *The Flame of Attention*. Hot off the presses she said. That evening I had a lot of work to do, but I couldn't put his book down. A chapter discussing the central Krishnamurti theme of "unobstructed awareness" riveted my attention.

Unobstructed awareness is pure *seeing* in the moment, without any interference whatever—no conditioned responses, no judgment, no liking or disliking, no desire for change, no motive, no attitude, no opinion, in fact no preconceived self. Just pure awareness.

The next morning during meditation I had one of the most profound experiences of my life. Without even thinking about it I slipped into a state of clear awareness. Suddenly I could look at anything in my life, even things I'd normally regard with fear or shame or embarrassment, without any reaction at all, just keen interest. There wasn't an atom of the universe I wanted to change. I was simply in the flow of *what is*. I felt utterly free, unencumbered, unobstructed. Joyously free. Later I realized that this experience, which lasted for ten or fifteen minutes, was overflowing with love.

I've always suspected that this extraordinary happening was the residual effect of my being in the transcendent presence of Krishnamurti the day before. While we were chatting some deeper communion must have occurred.

There are states of being which beggar the imagination, which lift us beyond our habitual routines of thinking and allow us a glimpse of divine wholeness. Perhaps we can enhance our everyday living with the blessing of these moments of grace.

Having learned so much from Krishnamurti, I should clarify the statement that spiritual teachers come to teach what cannot be taught. Even Jesus, whom Christians believe is the Son of God, did not succeed in transforming humanity. The Holy Land and so much of our world are still torn apart by hatred and violence. Jesus did his work. We have yet to do ours.

A great teacher has no interest in being followed or worshiped or even believed. A great teacher invites skepticism, questioning, challenge, provocation. A great teacher wants only to wake you up (and has no investment in that either).

A great teacher can suggest possibilities, can point toward truth, can be radiant with love. A great teacher can by his or her presence induct us into holy energies for a moment. But a great teacher will never trespass upon your own discovery of the sacred. Only you may step into the sanctuary of your own heart. Only you can awaken to the presence of God's wholeness right there within your own being.

FINDING HEAVEN

I have a theory that ideally actors should remain totally unknown to their public so they can be completely convincing as the various characters they play. The less the audience knows about us personally, the more likely they are to believe and be moved by our performances in the fantasies of particular plays or movies.

When Jonathan Miller, the director of our Los Angeles production of *Richard II*, spoke about the total commitment actors must give to our acting, he said that when audience members come backstage to greet us, all they should find in the dressing room is a little pile of ash.

Unfortunately, show biz is set up in such a way that to succeed a performer requires fame, which in turn requires constant exposure in the media. The anonymous seldom star in movies.

Actors must learn to create *two* forms of illusion: one to manifest the fictional characters we play in theater and films, and another for building and sustaining our semifictional public image. It's all part of the show.

For an actor like me, who believed it necessary to hide aspects of his everyday self from public view, the perpetual crafting of my public image was arduously tricky. I had to be constantly on guard during endless press and TV interviews. I didn't want to slip up and reveal my real self, especially when the inevitable questions, such as "Why aren't you married?" and "Don't you want children?" were asked with their covert yet obvious implications.

The care and protection of my partly fabricated public persona became a built-in, habitual part of myself along with the fear of exposure that I worried might stop my career cold.

For forty wonderful years I played romantic leading men and audiences responded to me, sometimes even *loved* me as these characters. I felt gratefully obligated to sustain their illusions as best I could in my consequently veiled real life.

Living as a somewhat fictional persona in public, every day, every week, every year, inevitably sloshed untruth into my private life. Even my long and deeply loving relationships with Martin and with our close friends were inhibited by my continuing unease about my sexuality, by my perpetual fear of exposure to public prejudice. This continued even after several outings in the rags. I was still placing my well-being in the hands of what I imagined to be that unruly crowd out there.

Then one hot, sunny afternoon in the summer of 2002 a minor miracle happened. My longtime friends Nancy and Sam were driving me to a dinner party and an interesting and unexpectedly enlightening discussion developed. We were wondering if I should or shouldn't discuss being gay in this book. My worry was the probability that all the subsequent interviews and reviews publicizing the book would then center on this "shocking admission" rather than on the spiritual themes of God, love, and forgiveness. I also worried that since I had never before discussed gay issues in public, I might get tripped up and discombobulated by my old fears.

Sam suggested that we stage a trial interview with Nancy (who was driving, but game) taking the part of the formidable Barbara Walters.

As "Barbara" asked some formerly scary questions like "Don't you feel that by going public in this way you'll be disappointing and hurting a lot of your loyal and loving fans?," all at once I unexpectedly opened within myself to a place I'd never experienced before under fire. I dropped any hint of the self-image I'd fought to protect for so many years. I dropped any preconceived agenda for the interview and simply listened carefully to the question and its implications, noticed my reactions, and then quietly listened within *myself* for the response. Suddenly my only interest was in the truth, whatever that might be. I lost all need to "spin" my answer to make myself look good or to pretend anything. I told "Barbara" that I'd kept silent about my sexual orientation all those decades partly because I was actually prejudiced against *myself*, and partly out of a desperate fear that honesty would have vanquished my career. I said that like all actors I was a practitioner of illusion, and I respected the rather sweet and even passionate illusions the audience had about me. (Even Mel Gibson, Brad Pitt, and Russell Crowe, all presumably straight, are in fact personally unknown to their adoring fans.) Further, now that the time has finally come for me to learn to love *what is*, maybe this is an opportunity for my fans to do the same.

This utterly novel experience of complete trust in the truth, in myself exactly as I was, in "Barbara" exactly as she was, and in the world exactly as it was, was like finding myself smack in the middle of heaven. A lifetime of constricting fears vanished in a sweet breeze of grace. The constant background static of my self-deprecatory inner monologue faded into silence.

I felt as if a malign aspect of myself that I had been born with finally released me. In my suddenly silent self I found all the warmth and love I'd worked so hard to cajole from the world outside. For the first time ever I felt easily confident in the integrity of my life. At long last I am free to be the part of God that God wanted me to be.

Heaven *is* truth. At long last I can *just be* (as Nana suggested so long ago). As long as I keep open and aware of *what is*, right now in the present, I can be a human among my fellow humans, with no reason to close my heart to love. Well into my sixties, I have finally made friends with life. The terrible weight of my fear simply disappeared like waking from a dark dream; I had nothing to prove anymore. Truth *is* heaven, and it's right here within us and in front of us always. Truth never avoids us, we avoid it. And in avoiding or altering the truth of who and what we are at any given moment, we invariably avoid love, awareness, freedom, and joy. Freedom dwells only in truth, as does love, as does change.

There *is* a trick to this truth game. The important lesson in all this is not about revealing secrets. The real challenge is in daring to brave the silence and trust the invisible presence within each of us. Perception of the true requires not only inner silence, but also a moment of emptiness—being empty of preconceived ideas of what we want the truth to be, emptiness of desire and motive and any agenda—certainly emptiness of one's accumulated self-image. The idea of experiencing this silent emptiness while listening for truth can seem mortally fearsome— it is a momentary death of the "self"—it is a surrender of what we *think* we want to the actual fact—it is an openness to and complete trust of one's deeper self and of life. This detachment from the past, this complete lack of control, seems terrifying until it's actually experienced. When you *do* allow yourself to experience this alert emptiness, you'll find yourself in a place of trust and insight, and truth will arise with simplicity and grace.

INTIMATIONS OF ETERNITY

Last week I was sitting with some friends on the lawn behind my beach house looking out over the Pacific. It was sunset time—the big event of the day. We were sipping mai tais and enjoying the immense beauty of the early evening, which had made us all rather quiet.

As the color-drenched sky began to darken enough to reveal one or two faint stars (that had been there all along), my friends wandered into the house to start making dinner.

I lingered alone by the sea watching the majestic retreat of the sun. The sea was in a gentle mood, its tiny waves barely disturbing the reef's tide pools. A school of small fish flashed up out of the shallow water all at once and disappeared, then leaped again, perhaps being chased by a predator or maybe just fooling around. Orange clouds reflected reddish ripples on the blue-green water.

Watching all this, I seemed for a few moments to disappear. There was only seeing. And an unusual dimension of consciousness opened. I remembered sitting on the wall under the walnut tree as a child and "seeing" for the very first time. It seemed clear to me in this silent moment that my personal worries and strivings, my desires for approval and fulfillment and fame, my sense of being a separate, competitive entity were in fact rather moot and trivial, strangely irrelevant in the timeless wholeness of eternal reality. It was briefly clear to me that there is vastly more to living than we're usually aware of.

We're used to thinking of the sacred as something set apart in a heavenly realm to be worshiped from afar. We invent distant deities who judge, reward, and punish us. We give these deities omnipotent power and consequently we fear them (when we give ourselves time to think about them at all).

Wouldn't it be a splendid joke on us if the sacred wasn't distant and "other" in the least, if holiness in fact surrounded and infused every atom of the clamorous tumult of our everyday lives? What if God, rather than being the remote creator and judge of our strife-ridden world, *is* our world and our selves and everything that exists and everything beyond existence, too? What if, despite our fears to the contrary, we're ultimately *not* separate from sacredness, but wholly unified with each other and the divine? What if the only barrier between us and our realization of our own divinity is simply our ignorance?

ACKNOWLEDGMENTS

Having never before imagined myself writing a book, I'm grateful to Judith Regan for inviting me into the rich learning experience of doing so. And I'm immensely thankful for the editorial wisdom of Calvert Morgan.

I am happily beholden to Martin's prodigious memory, his galvanizing flashes of truth, and his indispensable organizational suggestions.

My thanks to Sam and Nancy for setting the stage for an epiphany that changed my life.

Warmest thanks to Andrew Harvey for his beautiful translation of "The World of Origin."

And my loving gratitude to Dr. Carolyn Conger for her heartfelt encouragement.